Stephen Hawes

Twayne's English Authors Series

Arthur F. Kinney, Editor
University of Massachusetts, Amherst

TEAS 354

HENRY VII OF ENGLAND
Frontispiece by Michiel Sittow.
*Courtesy of the National Portrait Gallery,
copyright reserved.*

Stephen Hawes

By A. S. G. Edwards

University of Victoria

Twayne Publishers • Boston

Stephen Hawes

A. S. G. Edwards

Copyright © 1983 by G.K. Hall & Company
All Rights Reserved
Published by Twayne Publishers
A Division of G. K. Hall & Company
70 Lincoln Street
Boston, Massachusetts 02111

Book Production by John Amburg

Book Design by Barbara Anderson

Printed on permanent/durable acid-free
paper and bound in the United States of
America.

**Library of Congress Cataloging in
Publication Data**

Edwards, A. S. G. (Anthony Stockwell
Garfield), 1942–
Stephen Hawes.

(Twayne's English authors series:
TEAS 354)
Bibliography: p. 119
Includes index.
1. Hawes, Stephen, d. 1523?
—Criticism and interpretation.
I. Title. II. Series.
PR2291.E36   1983   821'.2   82-16048
ISBN 0-8057-6840-8

Contents

About the Author
Editor's Note
Preface
Acknowledgments
Chronology

> *Chapter One*
> The Poet and His Milieu   1
>
> *Chapter Two*
> *The Pastime of Pleasure*   26
>
> *Chapter Three*
> The Minor Poems   59
>
> *Chapter Four*
> Reputation, Influence, and Achievement   88

Notes and References   109
Selected Bibliography   119
Index   126

About the Author

Anthony S. G. Edwards was educated at Reading, McMaster, and London universities. He is currently Associate Professor and Director of Graduate Studies in the Department of English, University of Victoria, B.C., Canada. He is General Editor of the Index of Middle English Prose and of the Garland Medieval Text Series, Advisory Editor to *Analytical & Enumerative Bibliography,* on the Advisory Boards of *Review* and *Text,* and Secretary of the Renaissance English Text Society. He has edited George Cavendish's *Metrical Visions, John Skelton: The Critical Heritage*, and (with D. Pearsall) *Middle English Prose: Essays on Bibliographical Problems.* His articles and reviews have appeared in a number of scholarly journals.

Editor's Note

As a poet in the court of Henry VII, Stephen Hawes was a harbinger of essential trends in Renaissance poetry. "He possessed," wrote John Bale, "an ingenious mind." In this first full-length study of his life and work based on manuscripts and early editions as well as the 1974 edition of his minor poems, A. S. G. Edwards shows how Hawes's struggling poetic experiments—until now dismissed because of their heavy use of allegory, apparent obscurity, or metrical weaknesses—conceal a thoughtful and original writer whose work is sometimes surprisingly personal, courageously political, or technically innovative; he is at least as modern as he is medieval in case of mind and in literary achievement. His work with Wynkyn de Worde fusing poems and woodcuts, moreover, anticipates emblem books and emblem poetry in England by nearly a century. To understand Hawes as Edwards understands him is to discover new roots for major characteristics of the English Renaissance. This is an important and stimulating study.

Arthur F. Kinney

Preface

This is the first book-length study ever published of Stephen Hawes's poetry. There are considerable difficulties in undertaking it, not the least of which is the critical dismissal of Hawes (with one or two notable exceptions) over the centuries. It is no part of my intention to maintain that he is a genius whose work should be dramatically reevaluated. Hawes is a minor poet, in terms of the quality and volume of his output. I shall not seek to claim otherwise.

But it is possible for a minor poet to have both intrinsic interest and historical importance. Hawes, as I will try to show, is, in some respects, far more effective and innovative as a poet than has often been allowed in the past. Constructive evaluation of his work depends in the first place on an understanding of what he was trying to do. I have attempted to establish the literary and historical contexts for Hawes's poetry. I have also tried to define those elements in his poetic which derive from literary tradition. With such perspectives it is possible to argue that Hawes is within limits a thoughtful, innovative poet seeking to explore new techniques and new poetic material.

In many ways this is a preliminary study. We still lack any responsible study of Hawes's sources and his treatment of them. Far more work needs to be done on Hawes's use of iconographic tradition, to continue and extend the work so brilliantly begun in Samuel Chew's *The Pilgrimage of Life* (New Haven, 1962). And we still need to know far more about Hawes's role within the court of Henry VII. Such research would provide a firm basis for an assessment of Hawes's place and achievement in literary history.

I have been particularly fortunate in my Field Editor, Arthur F. Kinney, who has given me generous advice and encouragement. I am indebted to the University of Victoria for a Research Grant to assist in the completion of this book, and to my secretary, Mrs. B. Grillowitzer, for imposing order on a difficult manuscript with her usual composure and intelligence.

A. S. G. Edwards

University of Victoria

Acknowledgments

Some sentences from chapter 1 first appeared in *Gutenberg Jahrbuch* (Mainz, 1980); some sentences from chapter 4 first appeared in *Notes & Queries* (Oxford: Oxford University Press, 1979). The frontispiece appears by permission of the National Portrait Gallery.

Chronology

1470–1475   Hawes's likely birth (exact date unknown).

1485   Henry VII ascends to the throne.

1493   Hawes possibly at Magdalen College, Oxford.

1503   Hawes at Henry VII's court; receives an allowance to buy mourning for the queen's death.

1503–1504   *Example of Virtue* written.

1505–1506   *Pastime of Pleasure* written.

1506   Receives payment from Henry VII for a "ballet."

1509   *Example of Virtue, Pastime of Pleasure, Conversion of Swearers,* and *A Joyful Meditation* all published. Deaths of Margaret Beaufort and Henry VII; accession of Henry VIII.

1510–1511   *Comfort of Lovers* written.

1515   *Comfort of Lovers* published.

ca. 1529   Thomas Feylde laments Hawes's death in *A Contrauersye bytwene a louer and a laye.*

1530   Robert Copland laments Hawes's death in de Worde's edition of *The assemble of fowles.*

Chapter One

The Poet and His Milieu

Life and Works

The details of Stephen Hawes's life are shrouded in obscurity. The earliest biography of him appeared more than a generation after his probable death. Bishop John Bale wrote in 1557 that

Stephen Hawes, a man of distinguished family, was eager from his youth to develop his mind through humane studies. Having left his family he went to various universities in different countries to seek to become a man of letters. Through study in England, Scotland and France he carefully acquired sophistication in his speech, manners and personal habits. He possessed an ingenious mind; and all his life and utterance were dedicated to demonstrating that he was, as it were, an example of virtue. At length, that most illustrious prince, Henry VII, king of England, called him to his court, to his inner chamber and to his private counsels, on the sole recommendation of his virtue. While there, in the pleasant leisure of contemplation, he composed in English:

The Delight of the Spirit
The Comfort of Lovers
The Example of Virtue
Concerning the Marriage of the Prince
The Alphabet of Birds
The Temple of Glass

He composed a number of other works in verse and prose which were read by many with pleasure. He regained his reputation in 1500 under the reign of the aforesaid Henry.[1]

Subsequent research has done little to clarify the vagueness surrounding certain details in Bale's account. The date of Hawes's birth is unknown, but was possibly sometime in the 1470s (1475 is often suggested). Details of his parentage and education are lacking. He may be the same "Stephen Haugh" who is identified as son and heir of John Haugh, late a justice of the Common Bench in Norfolk in 1506.[2] It seems possible that he attended the University of Oxford as a member of Magdalen College in 1493.[3] It is not known where (or, indeed, whether) he studied in Scotland and France.

One of the few claims in Bale's account that can be verified is that Hawes was a member of the court of Henry VII. All his works published in Henry's reign described him as "groom of the chamber" to the king. Official records of various payments to him survive, the earliest dating from 1503, which confirm him as a member of Henry's retinue. The latest of these payments occurred in early 1506 and is noteworthy as the earliest specific identification of Hawes as a poet. In January of that year he was paid ten shillings from the King's Book of Payments "for a ballet that he gave to the kings grace in rewarde."[4]

Hawes's life from this point is almost wholly conjecture. Matters are complicated by the fact that the name Hawes was a common one in East Anglia in the early sixteenth century. Some attempts have been made to identify him with a Stephen Hawes who received the rectory of Withern in Lincolnshire in January 1507/8. But this is based on a confusion over the death of this candidate who was deceased before Hawes composed his last known work, *The Comfort of Lovers*.[5] He is described in this work as "somtyme grome of yᵉ honourable chambre of our late souerayne lorde kynge Henry yᵉ seuenth," which suggests that he had not gained a position in the court of Henry VIII. The poem itself contains obscure allusions to what appear to be personal difficulties with men of noble rank. All that is certain is that he was dead by 1529 when Thomas Feylde in his poem *A Contrauersye bytwene a louer and a laye* alludes to "Yonge Steuen Hawse whose soule god pardon."

Most but not all of Hawes's works listed by Bale have survived. All are poems, and with the exception of the *Comfort of Lovers* they seem to have been first published in the same year. Hawes's greatest work, his *Pastime of Pleasure* (? Bale's "Delight of the Spirit") appeared in 1509, as did *Example of Virtue* and *Joyful Meditation,* together with the *Conversion of Swearers,* works not mentioned by Bale. Of the other three works mentioned by Bale, one, *The Temple of Glass,* is in fact by Lydgate and the others, the *Alphabet of Birds* and *Concerning the marriage of the Prince,* cannot be identified. No prose works survive, and attempts to add to the canon of Hawes's poetry have been unconvincing.[6]

The only other certain information about Hawes's life and work can be gleaned from his own poems. We gather that two of them were written some time before their actual publication. The introduction of the *Example of Virtue* states that it was written in the "xix yeare" of Henry VII, which would place it between August 1503 and August 1504. A similar note in the *Pastime of Pleasure* dates its composition in the "xxi yeare" of Henry's reign, that is, between August 1505 and August 1506. The *Comfort of Lovers* is described on its title page as written "in the seconde yere of the reygne of . . . kynge Henry the eyght"—between April 1510 and April 1511. The only surviving edition of this work is later, dating apparently from 1515.

Occasional attempts have been made to see autobiographical significance to assertions made in the course of Hawes's poems.[7] For example, Graunde Amour, the hero of the *Pastime of Pleasure*, states at one point: "I thought me past all chyldly ygnoraunce / The .xxj. yere of my yonge flourynge aege" (3053–54). Scholars have sought to derive Hawes's own birthdate from this pronouncement. But it is not clear how it can be reconciled with the assertion made two years earlier in the *Example of Virtue* by the hero that "By this tyme was I .lx. yere old" (1864). Such attempts seem unprofitable. There are possibly some topical allusions in Hawes's poetry, and very probably some autobiographical references in *The Comfort of Lovers* (which will be discussed in chapter 3). But little certain information about Hawes's life emerges from his poems.

Hawes is a shadowy figure. We can only attempt to flesh out the meager information we have about him by relating him to various contexts that will help us better to understand the circumstances and motives that surround the creation of his poems.

Hawes and Henry VII: Literature and the Court

As we have already seen, virtually the only fact we have about Hawes's life is that he was a member of Henry VII's court. We have no certain idea of what duties were attached to the office of groom of the Privy Chamber. But it is reasonable to assume that his role was connected with his poetic activities. Apart from the recorded payment to him specifically for a "ballet" for the King in 1506 it is clear that one of the functions of the Privy Chamber, as it developed under successive English kings, was to provide a focus for literary, cultural, and educational impulses within the court circle.[8]

But Henry VII was unusual in that he included in his court circle a number of men of letters and gave several of them positions of authority. And some of his advisors and intimates followed his example. His reasons for employing such men were deeply practical.

In 1485 Henry had become king of England as a result of his victory over Richard III at Bosworth Field. The kingdom he had won was one divided and enfeebled by the internecine struggles of the Wars of the Roses, which had gone on for over thirty years between the contending houses of York and Lancaster. At the time of his accession there was little to suggest that Henry had a much better chance than his predecessor in establishing firm control over his kingdom and mending the bitter divisions of decades.

In fact Henry proved to be a ruler of great acumen. A Lancastrian monarch, his first conciliatory act was to marry Elizabeth of York. As Hawes puts it in *The Example of Virtue,*

> The whyte rose [of York] that with tempestes troublous
> Aualed was and eke blowen asyde
> The reed rose [of Lancaster] fortyfyed and made
>   delycyous . . .
> Thus god by grace dyd well combyne
> The rede rose and the whyte in maryage.
>   (2081–83, 2088–89)

Subsequent acts were equally astute. He restored the largely ruined economy, firmly suppressed internal conflict, and established England as an international force. The kingdom he bequeathed to his son, Henry VIII, was affluent, stable, and powerful.[9]

Such a transformation was not easily achieved. The early years of Henry's reign were marked by the attempted usurpations of the pretenders Lambert Simnel and Perkin Warbeck, as well as other threats to his kingdom's stability. Henry overcame all such challenges. But he remained conscious of the need to demonstrate both the legitimacy of his rule and the nature of his achievements. He was quick to perceive the potential of word and image to assist him in such demonstrations.

Several figures appear to have been employed in Henry's court to employ their literary talents for political ends. One such was Bernard André, a French poet who accompanied Henry when he returned from France in 1485. He seems to have been an official apologist and publicist for the king. He wrote several works in praise of him: *Les Douze triomphes de Henry VII,* the *Vita Henrici VII,* and a series of *Annales Henrici VII.* He also composed a number of poems celebrating particular events. The records of Henry's reign show that he was well rewarded for his activities.[10]

André was not alone in being employed by the king to serve as a propagandist for his cause. A characteristic of Henry's reign was his frequent commissioning of formal pageants to mark significant events, such as his marriage or the betrothal of his eldest son, Arthur. Such pageants were designed to reflect, through their language and iconography, the underlying political significance of the events they celebrated. Two figures who were particularly active in creating these pageants were John English and William Cornish. Little is known about the former, beyond the fact that he was Master of the King's Players in 1501, from which time details of a number of his elaborate revels survive. Rather more is known about Cornish. It seems likely that from the 1490s he was responsible for the creation of a number of court festivals or "disguisings" which had clear political implications.[11]

Such figures as André, English, and Cornish demonstrate the most obvious way in which Henry VII employed men of letters within his court: as propagandists and apologists for his rule. Others were employed in ways that were more complex. The most distinguished writer in Henry's court was the poet John Skelton. Created poet-laureate by three universities, acclaimed as a scholar, Skelton came to court as tutor to the king's son, the future Henry VIII. While so employed he wrote two works which reflect his apparent sense of the implications of his role. The first is his *Speculum Principis,* a didactic treatise on the nature and conduct of the kingly office, written in Latin prose. This survives only in a single manuscript, presumably prepared for his charge. The other is his *Bouge of Court,* a verse dream allegory in English, which satirizes the greedy and sycophantic postures of various kinds of courtiers. This was printed by Wynkyn de Worde in 1498. For Skelton, the role of tutor seems to have encompassed both private counsel and public criticism of court life.[12]

A fringe figure of some relevance to Hawes was the priest poet Alexander Barclay, who produced a number of verse translations. His version of the *Miseria Curialium* of Aenius Sylvius contains the first eclogues written in English. These include allusions to various members of the court circle, including Henry VII himself. Barclay's position (if any) within the court is impossible to define. But as we will see, he certainly knew Skelton's poems and quite possibly Hawes's.[13]

There were, then, clear connections between literary and political activities within Henry's own household, connections which go some way toward explaining Hawes's presence as a groom of the Privy Chamber. Henry was not alone in encouraging men of literary talent for his own purposes. Other members of the court seem to have been equally concerned to promote such men. One such was John Morton, archbishop of Canterbury. His entourage included as chaplain the poet and dramatist Henry Medwall and the young Thomas More, whose initial reputation seems to have derived in some measure from his skill as a poet.[14]

A figure of even greater prestige and influence than Morton in promoting literary activity was Henry VII's mother, Margaret Beaufort. Margaret's interest in vernacular literature manifested itself in various ways. She seems to have possessed a relatively large collection of English books. She translated devotional works into English, including parts of Thomas à Kempis's *Imitatio Christi* and a work entitled *The mirrour of golde for the sinful soul*. She also seems to have acted as patroness to translators of other didactic works, including Henry Watson's *Ship of Fools* and an edition of *Kynge Richarde*. Both these works as well as the *Imitatio Christi* were published by Wynkyn de Worde. De Worde also seems to have published at her request an edition of Walter Hilton's *Scale of Perfection* and a number of devotional tracts by her confessor, John Fisher, bishop of Rochester.[15]

Margaret is of potential relevance to an account of Hawes, for it has been suggested that she was in some way instrumental in encouraging de Worde to publish his poems.[16] Such a suggestion is a plausible one. She had an evidently close connection with de Worde who describes himself in the colophon to Hawes's *Conversion of Swearers* as "prynter vnto ye moost excellent pryncesse my lady the kynges graundame." She evidently shared Hawes's often-professed admiration for John Lydgate, to the extent of possessing copies of several of his works.[17] It is possible to discern an interest in vernacular poetry among members of her entourage. And Hawes himself speaks of her in admiring terms near the end of his *Example of Virtue* (2060–66). His naturally didactic tendencies might well have earned her favor.

But about this, as about so much else concerning Hawes's life, it is impossible to speak with any certainty. A few tantalizing hints do suggest, however, that Hawes's time as a court poet was not free from controversy, whoever his patrons were. Indeed, infighting, whether between poets or between poets and fellow courtiers, seems to have been not uncommon during the reigns of Henry VII and Henry VIII.

Barclay, for example, makes an explicit attack on Skelton and his poem *Philip Sparrow* in his *Ship of Fools* (1509). He also seems to attack him obliquely and at greater length in his Fourth Eclogue, and possibly in a further work now lost.[18] Skelton was involved in another satiric "flyting" with a fellow courtier, Christopher Garnesche, against whom he wrote a series of four satires in 1514.

The combative propensities of Barclay and Skelton are of some interest since they may have been involved in feuds with Hawes. Barclay's first Eclogue has the following passage:

> For Godfrey Gormand lately did me blame
> And as for him selfe, though he be gay and stoute,
> He hath nought but foly within and eke without . . .
> Because he alway maligneth against me,
> It playne appereth our life doth not agree.
>
> (838–40, 845–46)

"Godfrey Gormand" is apparently a disliked contemporary. It is tempting to suppose that some allusion to Hawes is intended here through the parallels between his name and that of Godfrey Gobelive, the grotesque dwarf who appears in the *Pastime of Pleasure*.[19] Such an oblique allusion is not implausible since Barclay alludes in equally cryptic terms to other court poets, including Cornish, in his eclogues.

The likelihood that Hawes was involved in some controversy within the court is strengthened by another allusion, this time by Skelton.

During the course of one of his attacks on Garnesche he alludes to "gorbellyd Godfrey," apparently one of Garnesche's associates.[20] Once again, it is tempting to link the allusion to Godfrey Gobelive, and, by extension to Hawes, his creator. Hawes and Skelton must certainly have known each other. And there are some possible allusions to Skelton in Hawes's *Comfort of Lovers*.[21]

But this is all speculation. It is helpful, however, in that it draws attention to another aspect of the milieu in which Hawes wrote. He was surrounded by a great deal of vigorous poetic activity and competition for courtly patronage. After the deaths of Margaret Beaufort and Henry VII in 1509 he seems to have lost favor under the new king, Henry VIII, and failed to gain a position at court. If the account of his affairs in the *Comfort of Lovers* can be adjudged autobiographical, efforts were made to prevent him from promulgating his verses. It is unclear whether this was due in any degree to the envy or malice of such an influential fellow poet as Skelton.

Such indications of Hawes's possible relationship to fellow poets are, it must be stressed, unsupported by any conclusive documentary evidence. But they may be of value if they serve to remind us that Hawes did not exist in poetic isolation. He was surrounded by a great deal of vigorous poetic activity and (probably) a considerable amount of competitiveness for patronage and the rewards it could bring.

It is necessary to discuss briefly a further aspect of Hawes's connection with the court and its implications for his poetry. Henry VII's reign saw the consolidation of an emergent fifteenth-century interest in humanism, in part through the king's selection of humanist scholars to fill important roles in his administration. Humanism had been brought to England by scholars who had traveled in Italy and Europe and been influenced by the revival of interest there in the classical tradition. Such scholars were prompted to bring both manuscripts and foreign humanists back to England to enable the dissemination of newly acquired knowledge. The primary impulse of humanist studies was initially educational. But it seems likely that its main appeal to Henry was practical. Humanist scholars provided him with a group of intelligent men capable of communicating in Latin, the common language of the late Middle Ages, men therefore of considerable practical worth to his administration.[22]

When the great Dutch humanist scholar Desiderius Erasmus visited England in 1499, he was struck by the wealth of humanist ability surrounding the king:

I find here a climate at once agreeable and extremely healthy, and such a quantity of intellectual refinement and scholarship, not of the usual pedantic and trivial kind either, but profound and learned and truly classical, in both Latin and Greek, that I have little longing left for Italy, except for the sake of visiting it. When I listen to Colet it seems to me that I am listening to Plato himself. Who could fail to be astonished at the universal scope of Grocyn's accomplishments? Could thing be more clever or profound or sophisticated than Linacre's mind? Did Nature ever create anything kinder, sweeter, or more harmonious than the character of Thomas More? But why need I rehearse the list further? marvellous to see what an extensive and rich crop of ancient learning is springing up here in England. . . .[23]

The names Erasmus cites suggest something of the links between humanism and Henry's court. John Colet was Dean of St. Paul's, a scholar and advisor to the king. He had been a student of William Grocyn, possibly the first great English humanist, under whom More also studied. He became Henry VII's personal physician and tutor to his son, Arthur. Thomas More was, as we have already seen, a member of the entourage of Bishop Morton, who was one of Henry's closest advisors. More already possessed a growing reputation both as scholar and poet. One may add to these the name of Skelton, poet and tutor to the future Henry VIII, whom Erasmus praised in the same year as "the light and glory of English letters," as well as a number of lesser luminaries.[24]

Most of these were men of affairs as well as scholars. Often they saw their learning as a practical tool, to be employed in their political activities. Such works as More's *Utopia,* for example, can be viewed as providing models for conduct within the body politic, as an expression of a direct experience of affairs of state.

As a member of the court Hawes must have had contact with such humanists. If, as seems possible, he had studied at Oxford, he may have been exposed to humanist thought even earlier. It seems appropriate to ask whether it has any implications for his poetry.

Such a question is not easy to answer. There are few direct indications of any knowledge of works that could be termed humanist. He may have known some of the works of Pindar,[25] but shows no conclusive knowledge of any classical authors. Possibly he knew the works of some of the medieval Italian humanists: it has been argued that Boccaccio's *De Genealogia Deorum* is used in the *Pastime of Pleasure*;[26] and Hawes clearly knew Petrarch's *Trionfi* in some form, although probably not directly.[27] But he does not evidence much acquaintance with or influence by works of humanist orientation.

It is possible that he may have absorbed some humanist attitudes. The most notable evidence of humanist sympathy is in his extended discussion of the practical usefulness of education for those in positions of political authority which he introduces into the *Pastime of Pleasure*.[28] But even here the education he prescribes is a clearly medieval one, involving the study of the trivium and quadrivium. What is unusual is that it is applied to a practical end.

There is little to suggest that Hawes was significantly affected by the humanist presence in Henry's court. He himself saw his prime poetic inspiration as deriving from the past in a very different way. It is to the question of the literary models and influences on Hawes that we must now turn.

Hawes and Poetic Tradition

Like many late medieval English poets Hawes appears conscious of his debt to his predecessors and expresses that consciousness in various ways in his writings.

Hawes's own acknowledgments of his indebtedness provide a starting point. He appeals in several of his poems to the medieval triumvirate of Chaucer, Gower, and Lydgate. At the beginning of the *Example of Virtue* he makes this avowal:

> O prudent Gower in langage pure
> Without corrupcyon moost facundyous
> O noble Chauser euer moost sure
> Of frutfull sentence ryght delycyous
> O vertuous Lydgat moche sentencyous

> Vnto you all I do me excuse
> Though I your connynge do now vse
> (22–28)

In his "prohemye" to the *Comfort of Lovers* he is a little more specific about the importance of this trio:

> First noble Gower moralytees dyde endyte
> And after hym Cauncers [i.e., Chaucer's] grete
>   bokes delectable
> Lyke a good phylosophre meruaylously dyde wryte
> After them Lydgate the monke commendable
> Made many wonderfull bokes moche profytable
> (22–26)

But it would be unwise to make too much of these and other similar allusions in Hawes's poetry. The conjunction of Chaucer, Gower, and Lydgate was, by Hawes's time, a conventional one. There are, in fact, very few indications of Chaucer's influence in Hawes's poems. His allusions to Gower show no certain acquaintance with his works.[29]

The question of Hawes's relationship to Lydgate is more complex. Lydgate is the one poet invoked in all of Hawes's works as example and inspiration. In two of his shorter poems, *The Conversion of Swearers* and *A Joyful Meditation,* he is the sole poetic example cited. And elsewhere Hawes's mention of Lydgate is differentiated both quantitatively and qualitatively from his praise of Chaucer and Gower. In the longest allusion to the three, in the *Pastime of Pleasure* (1317–1407), two lines are devoted to Gower, nineteen to Chaucer, and seventy to Lydgate. A similar emphasis can be found elsewhere when they are linked together, often coupled with an explicit acknowledgment of the example of Lydgate's art; for example, in the *Pastime of Pleasure*—

> O mayster Lydgate the moste dulcet sprynge
> Of famous rethoryke with balade ryall
> The chefe orygnall of my lernynge
> (1373–75)

—which Hawes aspires to commemorate in his own works:

> I lytell or nought expert in poetry
> Of my mayster Lydgate wyll folowe the trace
> As euermore so his name to magnyfy
> With suche lytell bokes by goddes grace
> Yf in this worlde I maye haue the space
> The lytell connynge that his grace me sent
> In tyme amonge in suche wyse shall be spent.
>   (1394–1400)

We can add the weight of tradition to testify to Hawes's admiration. Anthony à Wood, the seventeenth-century antiquary, seems to have been the first to record that Hawes was

highly esteemed by [Henry VII] for his facetious discourse, and prodigious memory; which last did evidently appear in this, that he could repeat by heart most of our English poets; especially Jo. Lydgate, a monk of Bury, whom he made equal, in some respects with Geff. Chaucer.[30]

If Wood's claim can be credited, then Hawes's memory must indeed have been prodigious, as a moment's reflection on Lydgate's poetic career makes clear. He was born around 1370. For much of his life he was resident as a Benedictine monk at the Abbey of Bury St. Edmund's. But his poetic reputation earned him the patronage of the most eminent of his contemporaries, including Henry V and Humphrey, duke of Gloucester. From the early years of the fifteenth century until his death about 1448 Lydgate produced an extraordinary quantity of verse in a diversity of genres. In his *Pastime of Pleasure* (1338–65) Hawes gives a partial indication of the range of his writings: his saint's lives, *The Life of Our Lady,* and *The Life of St. Edmund*; his *Fall of Princes,* an extended series of *de casibus* tragedies; the *Troy Book,* an historical epic; the brief, comic *Churl and the Bird*; and his dream vision, *The Temple of Glass.* These works represent only a portion of his total output, which has been conservatively estimated at over 150,000 lines.[31]

It is scarcely surprising that Hawes should have expressed admiration for Lydgate's works. These circulated extensively in manuscript down to his own time, and were also popular choices for the earliest English printers, Caxton and de Worde. But if the influence of Lydgate is readily explicable, what *forms* did that influence take? And how significant is this influence in terms of Hawes's poetry?

Once again, Hawes's own comments provide a starting point. Underlying his admiration for Lydgate seems to have been a sense of his distinctively *rhetorical* skills. At one point in the *Pastime* he talks revealingly about Lydgate's debt to classical tradition. He talks of "the well of fruytfulnesse / Whiche Vyrgyll claryfyed and also Tullyus / With latyn pure swete and delycyous" (1160–62), a tradition which he links directly to Lydgate's style:

> From whens my mayster Lydgate deryfyde
> The depured rethoryke in englysshe language
> To make our tongue so clerely puryfyed
> That the vyle termes shoulde nothynge arage
> As lyke a pye to chattre in a cage
> But for to speke with Rethoryke formally
> In the good ordre withouten vylany
>
>   (1163–69)

Hawes is praising Lydgate for a style that is deliberate and formalized, a contrast to the use of "vyle termes" in his employment of "depured rethoryke." This latter term has been taken to imply Hawes's conscious imitation of one of Lydgate's most distinctive stylistic features: the use of aureate diction.[32]

The term describes a style based in large measure on word choice, emphasizing the use of Latin-derived words, often polysyllabic ones.[33] The effect of such diction in Lydgate's poetry was (at its most successful) to create an elevated, sonorous style. Hawes himself seems to be thinking of this style (although he does not mention Lydgate) when he talks (in the *Pastime*) of

> Electynge wordes whiche are expedyent
> In latyn or in englysshe after the entent
> Encensynge out the aromatyke fume
> Our language rude to exyle and consume.
>
>   (921–24)

But Hawes's own debt to this aspect of Lydgatean style is perhaps less pronounced than his own comments and some recent criticism have implied. There is, admittedly, a degree of aureation in Hawes's longest poems, *The Example of Virtue* and the *Pastime of Pleasure*. Take, for example, this description from the *Pastime*:

> The rose was paynted with golden beames
> The wyndowes crystall clerely *claryfyde*
> The golden rayes and *depured* streames
> Of *radyant* Phebus that was *puryfyde*
> Ryght in the bull that tyme so *domysyde*
> Thrughe wyndowes was *resplendyshaunt*
> About the chambre fayre and *radyaunt.* . . .
>
> (1415–21)

All the italicized words could be termed "aureate" in that they are Latin-derived polysyllables. But this language seems to serve no real stylistic function. It is confined almost wholly to rhyme words.

In fact, it is only rarely that Hawes seeks to achieve an aureate style. The following lines (which have been singled out for criticism in the past)[34] seem to reflect some broader striving after a high style:

> Her redolente wordes of swete influence
> Degouted vapoure moost aromatyke
> And made conuersyon of my complacence
> Her depured and her lusty rethoryke
> My courage reformed that was so lunatyke.
>
> (5264–68)

But such lines are not typical of Hawes's style. As has been recently pointed out, one of the features of Hawes's style is a negative one, its "adjectival poverty."[35] It seems, however, that when he did seek adjectives he tended to employ ones that could be termed aureate, as evidenced by the two groups of lines just quoted. But such passages seem neither distinctive in themselves nor typical of Hawes's style. His own testimony is rather misleading in that it overemphasizes the presence of aureate diction in his verse.

Indeed, it might be more plausible to argue that Hawes's language achieves its most distinctive stylistic effects at those points at which it is most removed from Lydgate's elevated style. One thinks of the "low" couplet passages in the *Pastime of Pleasure,* or the unforced exhortation of his verse sermon, *The Conversion of Swearers.*

This is not to suggest that there is no evidence of any stylistic indebtedness on Hawes's part to Lydgate. But in general the parallels between the two lack any particular force. Hawes's language does contain a few Lydgatean words or phrases, but in number and frequency they are not compelling.[36]

There are some other features which probably derive from Lydgate, such as Hawes's astrological descriptions or his formal exclamations, or, indeed, his choice of "balade ryall" (*Pastime,* 1374) (i.e., rhyme royal) as the meter for most of his verse. He singles this form out for admiration in his praise of Lydgate.

There are some more specific indications of indebtedness to Lydgate on Hawes's part. For example, some of the balanced antitheses of parts of the *Comfort of Lovers* have distinctive parallels in one of Lydgate's minor poems:

> The more my payne the more my loue encreaseth
> The more my Ieopardy the truer is my harte
> The more I suffre the lesse the fyre releaseth
> The more I complayne the more is my smarte
> The more I se her the sharper is the darte
> The more I wryte the more my teeres dystyll
> The more I loue the hotter is my wyll.
>
> (638–44)

This seems to echo "Tyed With a Lyne," which begins:

> The more I go, the further I am behynde;
>   The further behynd, the nere the weyes end;
> The more I seche, the wers can I fynd.[37]

At some points Hawes attempts to combine *anaphora* (the beginning of a sequence of lines with the same word or words) with some rather ponderous wordplay, as in these lines from the *Pastime of Pleasure*:

> Mesure mesurynge mesuratly taketh
> Mesure mesurynge mesuratly dooth all
> Mesure mesurynge mesuratly maketh
> Mesure mesurynge mesuratly gyude shall.
> (2626–29)

This may reflect the influence of one of the most popular stanzas from Lydgate's *Fall of Princes,* which essays comparable verbal dexterity:

> Deceit deceyueth and shal be deceyued
> For be deceite who is deceyuable
> Though his deceitis be nat out parceyued
> To a deceyuour deceit is retournable.[38]

Such instances of Lydgate's apparent influence on Hawes do not add up to particularly striking evidence of indebtedness. One of the difficulties in any attempt to establish the degree of influence by one upon the other is that it tends to become a restricting and unrewarding exercise, for it focuses largely upon common deficiencies such as a cliché-ridden style and a tendency to expression of any utterance in trite proverbial commonplaces. In any enumeration of such shared faults Hawes is going to show to the greater disadvantage. Lydgate's poetic limitations are to some degree obscured by the vast bulk of his corpus (Hawes's oeuvre runs to less than ten thousand lines). What in Lydgate may serve to establish a crude homogeneity of style and tone becomes in Hawes stylistic and verbal poverty. It is more profitable simply to admit that Hawes has an impoverished poetic diction and a paucity of rhetorical resources and that these failings may as well be attributed to his reading of Lydgate as simply to native incapacity.

But if this area of inquiry is not particularly rewarding, the influence of Lydgate on Hawes does have another, more important aspect. He does provide a perspective on Hawes's poetic attitudes and concerns. For Hawes, Lydgate is the exemplar of the *moral* poet, "vertuous Lydgate," whose works are incitements to virtuous conduct. He praises Lydgate in such terms in several of his works; for example, in the *Pastime of Pleasure*:

> . . . my mayster Lydgate
> The monke of Bury dyde hym well apply
> Bothe to contryue and eke to translate
> And of vertue euer in especyally.
> (1338–41)

A similar view appears in *The Conversion of Swearers*:

> . . . my good mayster Lydgate
> The eloquent poete and monke of bery
> Dyde both contryue and also translate
> Many vertuous bookes to be in memorye
> Touchynge the trouthe well and sentencyously.
> (21–26)

Hawes's view of particular poems by Lydgate (or which he attributes to him) is also revealing; in *The Pastime of Pleasure*, *The Fall of Princes* is praised as "A good ensample for vs to dyspyse / This worlde so full of mutabylyte" (1349–50); *The Churl and the Bird* is "ryght gretely prouffytable" (1352); the *Assembly of Gods* is "a boke solacyous" (1363).

The perspective of this sort of praise of Lydgate becomes clearer when one contrasts it with Hawes's attitude toward the poetry of various (unnamed) contemporaries; he alludes to such poets a little later in the *Pastime* as those who

> But spend theyr tyme in vaynfull vanyte
> Makynge balades of feruent amyte
> As gestes and tryfles without fruytfulnes
> Thus all in vayne they spende theyr besynes.
> (1390–93)

It is not clear who Hawes has in mind here. He may well be referring to some aspect of the feuding among court poets already mentioned. But the comments are illuminating since they show how Hawes's preoccupation with Lydgate makes him see himself as conspicuously different as a poet from his contemporaries.

What is this sense of the role of the moral poet that Hawes seems to derive from Lydgate? Hawes's own claims as to the purpose of his poetry have, at times, a distinctly Lydgatean ring to them. He writes (he claims) to "eschewe ydelnesse" (*Pastime of Pleasure,* 44) or "to deuoyde ydlenes" (*Conversion of Swearers,* 47; *Comfort of Lovers,* 16). In this respect he makes clear his connection with "my mayster lydgate," who "in his lyfe the slouthe dyde eschewe / Makynge grete bokes to be in memory" (*Pastime,* 5812, 5814–15).

This connection expresses itself in more obvious ways, most distinctively in Hawes's choice of certain poetic modes which are obviously didactic: the verse homily in the *Conversion of Swearers*; didactic allegory in the *Pastime of Pleasure* and the *Example of Virtue.* In such respects the Lydgatean model is one naturally congruent with Hawes's sensibility.

More significant is the focus of these didactic concerns. Who is intended to profit from the "vertuous pastyme" of Hawes's writings? And in what ways? Once again, the model of Lydgate is helpful. The moral purpose of writing poetry is applied to the preservation of harmony and stability. At one point in the *Pastime* Hawes praises earlier poets "Whose famous draughtes . . . sette vs in ordre grace and gouernaunce" (894–95). He seems clearly to have in mind the trinity of Chaucer, Gower, and Lydgate. A little later he praises "these thre . . . whose famous draughtes no man can amende / The synne of slothe they dyde frome them dryue" (1366, 1368–69). He then goes on to single out Lydgate as "the chefe orygynall of my lernynge" (1375) in a lengthy accolade (1372–1407).

The passage is revealing in the stress it implicitly places on the moral example of Lydgate's poetry in establishing order within a world outside the poem. As we will see, Hawes writes with a clear sense of his poem's audience, so clear that his allusions to it (as in the case of the poets of "vaynfull vanyte") are often cryptic to the point of inaccessibility for a modern audience. And it seems that he saw his role as being like that of Lydgate—as a didactic advisor and counselor of those who commissioned his writings.

This sense of his role as advisor to the great in the Lydgate tradition is made most explicit in *A Joyful Meditation,* Hawes's poem on the accession of Henry VIII. The poem is in some respects a curious one (see chap. 3). But it does seem to represent some sort of bid by Hawes to

gain the favor of the new king. The prologue to his poem seeks to place
his own function as poet in an historical perspective. He invokes the
"gentyll poets in olde antyquyte" (2) who "wrote nothynge in vanyte /
But grounded them on good moralyte" (4–5). He singles out "The
ryght eloquent poete and monke of bery" (8) who he points out

> Made many fayre bookes . . .
> Presentynge his bookes gretely prouffytable
> To your worthy predecessour the .v. kynge Henry.
> (9, 12–13)

Hawes concludes by seeking to link himself to this tradition of moral
works addressed to kings:

> Wherfore good souerayne I beseche your hyghnes
> To pardon me whiche do rudely endyte . . .
> *In folowynge the monke whiche dyde nobly wryte*
> Besechynge your hyghnes and grace debonayre
> For to accepte this rude and lytell quayre.
> (22–23, 26–28; my italics)

The "monke" is, of course, Lydgate.

Hawes argues that "profitable books"—that is, those "grounded on
good morality"—were written by Lydgate for Henry VII's "worthy
predecessor," Henry V, just as he, Hawes, is now writing for Henry.
But Hawes's sense of the importance of Lydgate to him is clearly not
primarily a stylistic but an attitudinal one. He derives from Lydgate
this perception of the moral responsibility of the poet to counsel those
in positions of power and influence. Most of his works invoke such
figures: Henry VII in the *Pastime of Pleasure* and *Conversion of Swearers,*
Margaret Beaufort in the *Example of Virtue* and Henry VIII in *A Joyful
Meditation.* Only the enigmatic *Comfort of Lovers* does not have an overt
address to some such noble personage for reasons that we shall see later
(chap. 3).

Such an audience is, of course, unsurprising given what we have
already noted about Hawes's place within a courtly milieu. But it is
worth emphasizing that he saw his primary debt to the Lydgate
tradition as a responsibility to afford such an audience moral instruction

rather than propaganda, satire, or entertainment—uses for which other
poets were employed in the court circle. An important aspect of this
technique of instruction was Hawes's relationship with his printer,
Wynkyn de Worde.

Poet and Printer: Hawes and de Worde

Not all the influences on Hawes manifested themselves in such a
sense of a relationship to a tradition. His relationship with de Worde
shows that in some respects he was remarkably innovative in his
attempts to give poetic expression to that sense of a tradition.

Little is known about de Worde.[39] He appears to have been associated with William Caxton, England's first printer, before the
latter's return to England in 1476. After Caxton's death in 1491 or 1492
de Worde continued his workshop, printing a large number of works
until his own death in 1534.

All Hawes's poems were first published by de Worde. This is, in
itself, a sufficiently unusual feature of their relationship to warrant
comment, for, as has been noted, "as far as contemporary poets were
concerned [de Worde] made little attempt to cultivate a poet and
produce all his works."[40] He did publish single works by such poets as
Skelton, William Neville, and Thomas Feylde as well as some of
Alexander Barclay's translations. But Hawes is the only one de Worde
published in his entirety. In addition, he reprinted the *Pastime of
Pleasure,* the *Example of Virtue* (twice), and the *Conversion of Swearers.*

We do not know what drew de Worde to Hawes's work. The
likelihood is strong that it was some such noble patron as Margaret
Beaufort, as I have already suggested. What *is* clear is that the decision
to publish Hawes was not a hasty one. Although both the *Example of
Virtue* and the *Pastime of Pleasure* appeared in 1509, they had been
written much earlier (1503/4 and 1505/6, respectively). One of the
reasons for such delay in publication may have been that de Worde was
anxious to insure that there was an extremely close correlation between
the verbal and visual aspects of his editions. For it seems that for both
these texts de Worde sought to reflect through the accompanying
woodcuts the detail and significance of Hawes's poems.

Such an attempted correlation of the verbal and visual aspects of a
literary work is very unusual in early sixteenth-century publishing. But

it is clear that the attempt was deliberate and systematic. For example, in the *Pastime of Pleasure,* where some twenty-four separate woodcuts appear, it seems that at least twenty were probably commissioned specifically for the poem and reflect to a greater or lesser degree a detailed sensitivity to the poem. I have demonstrated this point in some detail elsewhere and will only offer brief illustrations here.[41]

A particularly interesting example comes at lines 3780–81 of the *Pastime,* which immediately precede a woodcut depicting the dwarf Godfrey Gobelive and the "olde mayden ryche" he is wooing. The lines read: "Lo here the fygures of them both certayne / Iuge whiche is best fauorde of them twayne." These lines obviously indicate that Hawes was aware of both the positioning and content of this woodcut when he was writing them. Even more interesting is the fact that the two figures in the woodcut are depicted with scrolls coming out of their mouths, reading (for Godfrey) "Fayre mayde wyll ye haue me," and (for the "mayde") "Nay syr for ye be yl fauored." These words are actually adaptations from lines in Hawes's poem, respectively: "Fayre mayd I sayd wyll ye me haue" (3768) and "Nay syr so god me kepe and saue / For you are euyll fauoured" (3769–70). The designer of the woodcut had access to Hawes's text and endeavored to incorporate it into his design. Such evidence suggests a very close collaboration between poet and printer to insure as exact a correspondence between text and picture as was possible.

One other example from the *Pastime* may suffice. It comes from the description of Time near the poem's conclusion. The text reads:

> And as dame fame was in laudacyon
> In to the temple with meruaylous lykenes
> Sodaynly came tyme in breuyacyon
> Whose symylytude I shall anone express
> Aged he was with a berde doubtles
> Of swalowes feders his wynges were longe
> His body fedred he was hye and stronge
>
> In his lefte hande he had an horology
> And in his ryght hande a fyre brennynge
> A swerde aboute hym gyrte full surely
> His legges armed clerely shynynge
> And on his noddle derkely flamynge

> Was sette Saturne pale as ony leed
> And Iupyter a myddes his forhed
>
> In the mouthe Mars / and in his ryght wynge
> Was splendent Phebus with his golden beames
> And in his brest there was resplendysshynge
> The shynynge Venus with depured streames
> That all about dyde cast her fyry leames
> In his left wynges Mercury / and aboue his wast
> Was horned Dyane her opposycyon past.
>
> (5607-27)

Once again, the woodcut artist is as faithful to the particulars of the text as the nature of his medium permits. The figure in the woodcut is bearded and has long feathered wings. He carries both a clock ("horology") and burning fire and bears a sword. His legs are covered in armor. The gods are represented by stars except for "splendent Phebus," who is depicted as the sun. All the stars appear in the positions specified in the text.

Such examples are typical of the relationship between text and woodcut in the *Pastime*. What is clear is that de Worde was remarkably concerned to insure that Hawes's poem was clearly complemented by its woodcuts. What makes such a concern all the more curious is that this was not the only occasion when de Worde appears to have been willing to put himself to the time, trouble, and expense of commissioning special woodcuts for the works of this previously unknown versifier.

For he had a completely new series of woodcuts designed for Hawes's *Example of Virtue*. The ten woodcuts in the series reveal, once again, that de Worde's artist was attempting to reflect Hawes's text, often with striking particularity. Thus early in the poem the hero is led into the presence of Dame Nature:

> Where that she sat as a fayre goddes
> All thynges creatynge by her besynes
>
> Me thought she was of merueylous beaute
> Tyll that Dyscrecyon lede me behynde
> Where that I sawe all the pryuyte
> Of her werke and humayne kynde

> And at her backe I dyd than fynde
> Of cruell deth a dolfull ymage
> That all her beaute dyd perswage.
>
> (517–25)

The accompanying woodcut reflects the sense and substance of this text with great fidelity. Nature is seated in the center; in front of her are two small children and small animals. Death stands behind her left shoulder; behind him are two dead humans and two dead animals. The visual dimension encapsulates and dramatizes the text of the poem.

Later in the same poem, there is an even closer correspondence between word and image. In his description of the King of Love, Hawes's poem reads:

> He had two wynges ryght large and grete
> And his body also was naked
> And a dart in his ryght hand was sette
> And a torche in his left hand brenned
> A botell aboute his necke was hanged
> His one leg armed and naked the other
> Hym for to se it was a wonder
>
> (1303–9)

Here again, the woodcut exactly mirrors the text, establishing that the artist had carefully read the poem before composing his design. In their overall effect the woodcuts in the *Example of Virtue* demonstrate once again a concern on de Worde's part to provide a coherent and consistent visual dimension to Hawes's verse.

There are few woodcuts in Hawes's other works de Worde printed. The single cuts in *A Joyful Meditation* and *The Comfort of Lovers* are quite general. But one of the two in the *Conversion of Swearers* shows the way in which Hawes was willing to exploit the potentiality of a visual image even when (as in this case) the woodcut had not been designed specifically for this poem. Near the conclusion of the *Conversion* he exhorts his audience to

> Beholde this lettre with the prynte also
> Of myn owne seale by perfyte portrayture
> Prynte it in mynde and ye shall helthe recure.
>
> (350–52)

The words suggest that Hawes was aware that a woodcut representing Christ and his thirteen sufferings was to appear in the poem, and uses it for an uncharacteristic play upon meanings of "print"—the relationship between seeing externally ("Beholde this lettre with the prynte") and comprehending internally ("Prynte it in mynde").

There are important implications of the relationship between Hawes and de Worde which enable us to arrive at a clearer understanding of the character and significance of his poetry. First, and most obvious, is Hawes's evident sense of the poem existing in a complementary relationship to other aspects of the printed book. He sees his text in a curiously modern way, in terms of its design within the overall book, taking account of the potential of woodcuts to enhance the significance of his verse.

Such a commitment to the printed book as a means of disseminating all his verse is itself unusual for the period. Few other poets of any degree of productivity seem to have chosen to have their works printed as a general practice. Some, indeed, such as Wyatt and Surrey, elected to have virtually none of their poetry published while they were alive. Their works circulated almost solely in manuscript. Other poets—Skelton is the obvious example—varied their mode of dissemination according to the subject matter of their verse.[42] But it seems very unusual for a court poet to have chosen print as the sole means of circulating his verse.[43]

The reasons for Hawes's decision can in part be found in the nature of his literary sensibility. The indications are that he formulated responses in primarily visual terms. The language of the *Pastime,* for example, is studded with terms like "pycture," "ymage," "depaynt" (i.e., "paint"), and a common resource in his poetry is descriptions of events set out on "clothe of aras," tapestries which depict narrative. Hawes's sensibility seems to have worked in such a localized, iconographic way, rather than in narrative sequences. Since his major poems are ostensibly narrative in design this poses some problems. But such problems are offset by intermittent passages of great success where the iconography achieves powerful poetic formulations.

It was, of course, natural that Hawes's sensibility would have led him to ally himself with a printer, to employ the resources of the woodcut to correlate with and give dramatic impact to his poetry. Some of his best effects, such as the conclusion of the *Pastime of Pleasure,* derive from such a successful correlation.

What is remarkable about this relationship between poet and printer is the degree to which it anticipates, in a previously unnoticed way, the nature of later emblem books, with their carefully integrated series of poems and images. But unlike the emblem books which are static series of such poems and images, Hawes sought to lend a new visual dimension to poetic narrative. This attempt to employ the full potentiality of printing resources in a secular text lacks parallels in the English publishing history of the period and points to one of the most unusual and innovative aspects of Hawes's art.

To sum up: Hawes was a court poet, unusual in the way in which his poetic instinct pulled him simultaneously forward and backward. He sought his poetic models and inspiration from the past, from the example of his "master" Lydgate. While he seems to have been largely untouched by the emergent humanism of the court, he does seem to have been in advance of his age in his perception of the potentiality of print. With such a preliminary sense of these aspects of his milieu we can now turn to a more detailed consideration of his poems.

Chapter Two
The Pastime of Pleasure

Hawes's *Pastime of Pleasure* was composed about 1505/6. Although this places it after his *Example of Virtue*, it is helpful to consider it first and separately. The *Pastime* is the longest and best known of his works. It also sheds much light on the poem that precedes it and those that follow.

Plot, Sources, and Analogues

The *Pastime of Pleasure* is Hawes's most ambitious poem in both length and scope. It opens with the narrator, Graunde Amour, walking in a meadow. He follows a path which brings him to an image indicating the alternative routes that lie before him: the Active or the Contemplative Life. He elects to pursue the Active Life and as he sets out on his path he meets Fame who tells him of the lady, La Belle Pucelle. Fame tells him he may seek to win her if he chooses to undertake a hazardous quest.

Graunde Amour agrees to follow this quest and is then directed to the Tower of Doctrine, where he receives extensive instruction in the Seven Liberal Arts: Grammar, Logic, Rhetoric, Arithmetic, Geometry, Music, and Astronomy. His studies are interrupted by an encounter with La Belle Pucelle before she returns to her own land.

Leaving the Tower of Doctrine, Graunde Amour goes to the Tower of Chivalry, where he is accepted into the court of King Melizius, who instructs him in the nature of knighthood. With his instruction complete he sets out on his quest, only to encounter a bizarre dwarf, Godfrey Gobelive, who recounts a series of antifeminist anecdotes. Graunde Amour parts company with the dwarf to visit Venus in her temple. She has a letter prepared to La Belle Pucelle in support of his love which Cupid delivers. On leaving her temple he again meets

Godfrey Gobelive, who is punished by Correction for his attacks on women.

Graunde Amour then continues his quest and confronts a series of opponents. He defeats a three-headed and then a seven-headed giant. Then he overcomes the monster of seven metals, finally to win La Belle Pucelle. The lovers are married and live happily until, aged and rich, Graunde Amour dies. In a concluding sequence, the Seven Deadly Sins, Time, the Nine Worthies, and then Eternity all appear over his grave offering admonitions and reflections.

Such a summary may indicate something of the difficulties the poem offers for a modern reader. One central difficulty is the remarkably heterogeneous quality of the different components of the poem's narrative. Hawes ranges from antifeminist satire in a "low" vein to elevated courtly dialogue, from didactic exposition to chivalric allegory. The fluctuations in tone and the changes in topic often seem imperfectly or unclearly related to the ostensible movement of the narrative, the love-quest of Graunde Amour for La Belle Pucelle.

It is not easy, when reading such a work, to develop responses in other than the most localized way. One is left rather with the sense of various tableaux being moved in front of the reader, which, whatever their impact as static entities, do not possess any accumulated meaning or significance but remain a jumble of unrelated scenes arbitrarily yoked into a narrative sequence. One way of dealing with this problem of response is to turn to literary history for guidance: to determine, that is, what sources exist for the poem that might account for the nature of its form and content.

Hawes himself offers few clues as to models for his poem. He does refer to a number of works during the course of it, but they are not of any help in understanding its design and purposes. Certainly there is little in the work of earlier major English writers that can be shown to have left any discernible literary impact on the *Pastime*. He does invoke the medieval triumvirate of vernacular poets, Chaucer, Gower, and Lydgate (1317–1407). But Hawes's debt to Chaucer is very slight, amounting to little more than occasional echoes.[1] Gower does not seem to have left any trace of his impact on the *Pastime*.[2] And Hawes's debt to Lydgate is, as we saw in chapter 1, primarily an attitudinal one. Nor does he seem to have read the greatest English prose romance, Malory's *Morte d'Arthur,* although this has occasionally been argued.[3]

Hawes does mention a few other works by name. He seems to have been aware of some romances and chronicles. He mentions the "recule of Troye" (236), doubtless Caxton's edition of the *Recuyell of the Histories of Troy* (1476). Elsewhere he refers to the tale of "Ponthus / Whiche loued Sydoyne" (1814–15), probably the early printed romance of *Sydoyne and Ponthus.* He also mentions the "cronycles of Spayne" (1030), a compilation that cannot be identified. Such allusions shed a little light on Hawes's cast of mind as apparent by his taste in literature but do not shed any light on the form of the *Pastime.*

Other posited sources prove to be equally unhelpful. Knowlton suggested that Hawes was influenced by Caxton's encyclopedic work, *The Mirror of the World,* published in 1481.[4] But there do not seem to be any convincing parallels. And as I suggested in chapter 1, Hawes's knowledge of humanist works or classical texts seems at best to have been slight and fragmented.

More promising as a model for the *Pastime* is the *Court of Sapience.* This is a fifteenth-century poem of some 2,300 lines, composed, like much of the *Pastime,* in rhyme royal stanzas. It was published by Caxton about 1481. The work has some broad correspondences with Hawes's poem: it is an allegory, cast in the form of a journey in which the protagonist seeks Sapience through whom he learns the message of Christian redemption. During the course of his journey to the court of Sapience he has numerous encounters, ·including a meeting, like Hawes's Graunde Amour, with the Seven Liberal Arts.

It seems clear that Hawes knew this poem. He mentions it in the *Pastime,* where he ascribes it erroneously to Lydgate.[5] And there are some verbal parallels between the two poems, as Wells has shown.[6] But Wells demonstrates that there is little *direct* influence by the *Court of Sapience* on the *Pastime.* Mainly the influence is filtered through Hawes's use of the work in his earlier *Example of Virtue.* Hence, the relationship to the *Pastime* is probably too diffuse to provide a useful model for Hawes's own poem.

Indeed, a general problem in any attempt to identify specific models or influences that may help to clarify the *Pastime* lies in the conventional nature of much of the material in his poem. Such aspects as the choice of two paths, the Seven Liberal Arts, the figures of Venus and Cupid, the Seven Deadly Sins, and the Nine Worthies are the most obvious examples of Hawes's use of traditional materials, materials with an extensive literary and/or iconographic tradition before the writing of the *Pastime*. I do not mean to suggest with one critic that the poem is therefore "a mere rifacimento of stock medieval motifs,"[7] but the accumulation of such conventional material does nothing to lessen the problems of response, both for a modern reader and quite possibly for Hawes's contemporary audience.

An understanding of medieval literary convention in the larger sense does, however, help to provide a degree of insight into the nature of Hawes's design in the *Pastime*. A number of the seemingly disparate elements in the poem assume a clearer relationship if viewed in terms of the medieval concept of the Pilgrimage of Life. The general preoccupation of much later medieval and early renaissance literature with the various aspects of man's journey through earthly life to salvation has been helpfully documented.[8] There existed prior to the *Pastime* an extensive tradition of writings that dealt in various ways with different aspects of this concern. Indeed, all the traditional motifs I enumerated in the previous paragraph have been shown to possess thematic relationships to the idea of the Pilgrimage of Life.

In trying to establish what *kind* of work the *Pastime* is, it is interesting to recall that recent scholarship has suggested that the Pilgrimage of Life may not be simply a concern reflected in medieval literature but may constitute a distinct literary genre in its own right.[9] Its first appearance came in the fourteenth century in the *Pelérinage de la Vie Humaine* by the French writer Guillaume de Deguileville.[10] This work is concerned with a quest in which the protagonist is given lengthy allegorical instruction in various aspects of Christian doctrine before embarking on a quest. During the course of his quest he encounters, among other perils, the Seven Deadly Sins, before reaching safety in the Ship of Religion.

Even in such a bald summary it can be seen there are suggestive parallels with the *Pastime*. In both works stress falls on extensive preliminary instruction in a predominantly allegorical mode, followed by a series of hazardous adventures and a climax that confronts the inevitable implications of earthly mortality. The *Pelérinage* is, moreover, a work that would have been accessible to Hawes. A prose version in Middle English was printed by Caxton in 1483. And a translation into English verse has been ascribed by Lydgate.[11]

It seems quite likely, then, that Hawes had some knowledge of previous literary formulations of the Pilgrimage of Life and that he was, at least to some degree, influenced by this form, at least insofar as his poem is concerned with quest, education, and mortality in conjunction. Such broad similarities with works in this genre are worth bearing in mind. But they constitute only one aspect, albeit a suggestive one, in the design of the *Pastime*. It is doubtful whether a specific model exists for Hawes's poem.

Allegory and Quest

Hawes does not appear to have felt constrained by the implication of the genre. In other works, such as the *Pelérinage,* the protagonist and the assemblage of allegorical figures he encounters individually possess certain specific moral or doctrinal significances that contribute to a definable didactic scheme within the work.

But in the *Pastime* allegory tends to function almost entirely at the level of personification. Graunde Amour *is* a lover; La Belle Pucelle *is* a beautiful maiden; and the quest *does* lead to a literal marriage. Character and event do not possess any concealed allegorical significance. This is not to say that everything in the poem is clear. At times allusions appear irrevocably obscure. One thinks, for example, of the oddly inserted hints on how Graunde Amour should deal with any of La Belle Pucelle's friends who are unfriendly to him (4683–4703). But such allusions are a problem of occasion and context, not of allegorical meaning.

Indeed, there seems to be a conscious effort to define Graunde Amour's activities in strictly literal terms, at least as they are represented in his quest for La Belle Pucelle. When, for example, he encounters the three-headed and seven-headed monsters, their heads are given certain symbolic attributes: falsehood, perjury, flattery, and so on. But these attributes are not linked to any articulated moral scheme. Instead, their significance is defined locally and specifically in relation to the situation of lovers, defining the hazards to love's fulfillment. For example,

> On the thryde heed in a baner square
> All of reed was wryten dyscomforte
> Causynge a louer for to drowne in care
> That he of loue shall haue no reporte
> But lokes hye his herte to transporte
> And I my selfe shall hym so assayle
> That he in loue shall nothynge preuayle.
> (4760–66)

Once again, the allegory is local and contextual, not schematic and/or doctrinal.

Only occasionally does Hawes attempt any more complex or systematic allegorical mode. And when he does do so the results are highly stereotyped. For example, he presents the traditional Christian allegory of the Pauline armor (Ephesians 6:11–18). But here he is simply drawing upon a parallel passage in his earlier *Example of Virtue* (1394–1401) which in its turn draws on a tradition of medieval writings on this theme.[12] Claims for any more elaborate or subtle allegory have been unconvincing. It has been suggested that in his description of the seven-metaled monster (5089–5116) Hawes is trying to make the metals correspond to the Seven Deadly Sins.[13] But there is nothing in the text to justify such a view. The point of the metals seems to be the way they protect Graunde Amour's adversary, hence making his ultimate victory all the more creditable.

In fact, Hawes's allegorical equations, such as they are, are generally quite straightforward. What is unusual is the way Hawes took a religious form and redeployed it so that much of the *Pastime* has a generically novel *secular* orientation. The actual nature of the quest Graunde Amour undertakes is defined from its outset as frankly secular. At the beginning of his journey Graunde Amour is confronted with the choice of "two hye wayes" (83). The alternatives are "the streyght waye of contemplacyon" (85) and "the waye of worldly dygnyte / Of the actyfe lyfe" (93–94). He chooses the life of "worldly dygnyte" rather than the life of renunciation implied in the alternative. It is worth noting that the very terms of the choice are unusual: "almost always Man is offered the option not between the Vita Contemplativa [the contemplative life] and the Vita Activa [the active life] but between

Virtue and Vice, Virtue and Pleasure."[14] Hawes eschews such conventional moral polarities, and in so doing he shifts the traditional emphasis of the Pilgrimage of Life. The quest acquires meaning not primarily from allegorical signification but from character and education. It is the figure of Graunde Amour and what he learns and becomes in pursuit of earthly love that is of central interest. The emphasis falls on the pursuit of activities defined as possessing significance within a limited, human world, not an idealized Christian one.

A couple of indications from the early sections of the *Pastime* may help to clarify this point. After making his decision to pursue the Active Life, Graunde Amour meets Fame, who tells him of La Belle Pucelle to such effect that "Her swete report so my herte set on fyre / With brennynge loue" (288–89). The decision to seek her out is presented as a reasoned choice on Graunde Amour's part:

> I haue determyned in my *Iugement*
> For la bell pucell the most fayre lady
> To passe the waye of so grete Ieopardy.
> (292–94; my italics)

The fact that he makes a considered, voluntary decision is once again a departure from tradition. In other works exploring the Pilgrimage of Life theme, the lover's quest generally appears as something imposed upon him, over which he has no control. He is, for example, often the victim of Cupid and his darts, which wound his heart with love.[15] Here the pursuit of love is deliberate, not involuntary, consistent with Graunde Amour's considered pursuit of the Active Life with the support of Fame.

Emphasis falls, then, on the operation of reason and secular aspiration in defining Graunde Amour's decision. But the choice of the Active Life is accompanied by some structural decisions which appear rather curious. In particular, Hawes seems to go to some lengths to prevent his audience's becoming at all engaged in the actual plot of his poem. We are assured at the outset that there is no doubt that Graunde Amour will be ultimately successful in achieving his quest. Before he has even started it he perceives in the "palays gloryous" of the Seven Liberal Arts a "cloth of aras" which portrays the various stages of his future quest and its eventual outcome. It concludes:

> How he weded the grete lady beauteous
> La bell pucell in her owne domynacyon
> After his labour and passage daungerous
> With solempne loye . . . well pyctured was
> In the fayre hall vpon the aras.
>
> (471–76)

From the beginning Hawes eschews the possibility of narrative suspense. The audience knows what will happen to Graunde Amour before he has undertaken anything. C. S. Lewis has pointed to this unusual aspect of the poem:

Before his pilgrim finishes his journey and wins La Bell Pucell we have that journey so frequently predicted that all suspense is lost; but then suspense is no part of his aim. . . .[16]

The statement is not wholly accurate—the end is not "frequently predicted"—although Hawes's hero occasionally talks anticipatorily of the end of his labors. But its central perception about the quest is valid and important. For if suspense is no part of Hawes's aim and his audience is deterred from becoming interested in Graunde Amour's quest per se, it seems appropriate to explore more closely the structure and design of the *Pastime*.

Rhetoric and the Responsibility of the Poet

What does happen to Graunde Amour? In relation to the length of the poem, not very much. The lack of suspense is accompanied by a curious lack of action. Much of the *Pastime* is not devoted directly to the pursuit of La Belle Pucelle at all. Graunde Amour's martial acts do not begin until chapter 33 (4270). And they are completed by the end of chapter 37 (5186). His deeds of chivalric prowess occupy less than 1,000 lines in a poem of over 5,800 lines. They constitute, moreover, the only significant physical action described in the poem.

It is a striking feature of the structure of the poem that by far the greatest amount of time, in numbers of lines, is spent in a lengthy sojourn at the Tower of Doctrine, where Graunde Amour is instructed by the Seven Liberal Arts. This episode occupies lines 372–1960 and

2549–2933 and is interrupted by his meeting with La Belle Pucelle. Much of the rest of the poem is devoted either to further instruction (at, for example, King Melizius's court) or to discussion. Hence, the narrative movement of the *Pastime* is extremely limited in terms of its overall length. It would seem that Hawes's chief concerns lie in areas that are apart from heroic narrative.

These concerns are reflected through a reworking and readjusting of the basic generic form of the Pilgrimage of Life. Onto this form Hawes grafts some new preoccupations which extend it in different directions and which serve to give a new orientation to his poem.

The first of these concerns can be broadly defined as educational. It seems that the process of the hero's education is of far greater concern to Hawes than its manifestation in direct action. His central focus for this educational concern is the extended discussion of the Seven Liberal Arts. The Arts formed the basis for the medieval educational system. Derived from the curriculum of ancient Greece, they had established themselves as an enduring codification of key aspects of learning in the Middle Ages and early Renaissance.[17] They formed a traditional part of the university curriculum. If, as seems likely, Hawes attended Oxford, he would have studied them there.

The Seven Liberal Arts were generally divided into the trivium, comprising grammar, rhetoric, and logic, and the quadrivium, comprising arithmetic, geometry, music, and astronomy. Hawes observes these divisions in the *Pastime,* enumerating first the trivium and then the quadrivium. But his discussion is curious in its emphases. There is no attempt to discuss each of the arts to anything like the same degree. Nearly two-thirds of Hawes's whole discussion of the trivium is devoted to a single one, rhetoric (652–1295). The remainder are treated in a relatively cursory manner, with little or no developed discussion.

This seeming lack of organization extends even into the way the arts are presented. They do not appear, as I have mentioned, in a single sequence. There is an interruption after the presentation of Arithmetic, which is hence separated from the other members of the quadrivium.[18] Interruptions also occur when Graunde Amour glimpses La Belle Pucelle (1450–1519) and when he meets Music (1520–80), speaks to her, and is afterwards consoled by Counsel (1581–2548). One does not get any clear sense of uniform significance or overall structure to the presentation of the Seven Liberal Arts. There is a perfunctory gesture toward a presentation of the whole system. But it is clear that Hawes's real concerns lie in very specific directions.

Clearly rhetoric is of primary interest to Hawes. The very length of his discussion invites such an assumption, if not the startlingly innovative nature of parts of his discussion of the subject. For we find here the first discussion in English of the terms of Ciceronian rhetoric[19] and quite probably the earliest English account of the art of memory.[20] But these significances are not part of our present concern. The basic question Hawes's discussion of rhetoric poses is its implications and relationship to the rest of the *Pastime.*

To attempt to answer this it is necessary to begin with Hawes's definition of the purposes of rhetoric:

> Rethoryke . . . was founde by reason
> Man for to gouerne well and prudently
> His wordes to ordre his speche to puryfy.
> (691–93)

That is, rhetoric is a rational way of imposing an ordered structure on human utterance. As he puts it a little later: "Without ordre without reason we clatter / Where is no reason it vayleth not to chatter" (865–66). This emphasis on the rational function underlying human speech becomes particularly relevant to the role of the poet. His purpose becomes a didactic and expository one, to exemplify right conduct by the way he writes:

> So famous poetes dyde vs endoctryne
> Of the ryght waye for to be intellectyfe
> Theyr fables they dyde ryght so ymagyne
> That by example we maye voyde the stryfe
> And without myschefe for to lede our lyfe
> By the aduertence of theyr storyes olde
> The fruyte werof we maye full well beholde.
> (1072–78)

Poetry, he suggests, in its proper function serves to demonstrate a moral purpose, the "ryght waye . . . for to lede our lyfe"; it is in this way that we profit from the example of works. But he makes a clear distinction between this function of the works of "famous poetes" with their "storyes olde" and situations in his own times. Contemporary poets lack this moral seriousness, and

> They fayne no fables pleasaunt and couerte
> But spend theyr tyme in vaynfull vanyte
> Makynge balades of feruent amyte
> As gestes and tryfles without fruytfulnes
> Thus all in vayne they spend theyr besynes.
>   (1389–93)

The result is a devaluation and depreciation of the nature and purpose of poetry:

> For now the people whiche is dull and rude
> Yf that they do rede a fatall scrypture
> And can not moralyse the semelytude
> Whiche to theyr wyttes is so harde and obscure
> Than wyll they saye that it is sene in vre
> That nought do poetes but depaynt and lye
> Deceyuynge them by tongues of flatery.
>   (806–12)

In spite of their rather cryptic nature these lines, in conjunction with the other passages just quoted, do help us to arrive at a clearer understanding of Hawes's sense of the proper purposes of poetry. Such poetry should ideally be "fables" (1074, 1389), particularly those which are "pleasaunt and couerte" (1389). This seems to mean that proper poetry is allegorical poetry. Hawes dismisses "balades" as merely "gestes" and "tryfles," unsuitable matter for serious readers of poetry. He complains of those who cannot read a "fatall scrypture" and "moralyze the semelytude."

One of the key words here is "fatall." It is one that was clearly important to Hawes and his theories about poetry. In the earlier *Example of Virtue,* for example, he speaks of

> poetes that were fatall
> Craftely colored with clowdy fygures
> The true sentence of all theyr scryptures.
>
> (901–3)

And at the beginning of the *Pastime* he praises his mentor Lydgate for producing

> Ryght famous bokes of parfyte memory
> Of his faynynge with termes eloquent
> Whos fatall fyccyons are yet permanent.
>
> (31–33)

True poetry is "fatal," a word that is generally glossed as "prophetic," but more properly in its contexts seems to mean "true" or "truthful." But such truths as he perceives cannot be overtly expressed. In the lines from the *Example of Virtue* quoted above he speaks of "clowdy fygures" as the proper mode for expressing "scryptures." The term appears in his praise of Lydgate, whose writings are "Grounded on reason with clowdy fygures / He cloked the trouthe of all his scryptures" (34–35). Similar views on the true nature of poetry can be found elsewhere in Hawes. At the beginning of the *Conversion of Swearers* he speaks of "ryght notable clerkes / Grounded on reason" (3–4) and "Specyally poetes vnder cloudy fygures / Coueryd the trouthe of all theyr scryptures" (13–14). And the *Comfort of Lovers* opens in similar fashion:

> The gentyll poetes vnder cloudy fygures
> Do touche a trouth and cloke it subtylly
> Harde is to construe poetycall scryptures
> They are so fayned & made sentencyously.
>
> (1–4)

What Hawes seems to be arguing for is the validity and importance of a form of allegorical poetry, a poetry in which meaning is concealed beneath "cloudy figures" of its surface, meaning which remains accessible only to the intelligent, thoughtful reader since it is "grounded on reason." Hawes stresses at the beginning of the *Pastime,* "I shall blowe

out a fume / To hyde my mynde vnderneth a fable / By conuert colour"
(40–42). A "fable" is "fatall fyccyon" possessing a concealed meaning, a
"colour":

> For under a colour a truthe maye aryse
> As was the guyse in olde antyquyte
> Of poetes olde.
>
> (50–52)

It is a paradox of the poem that the theoretical justification for the
importance of poetic allegory is far larger than the allegory itself, which
is, as I have said, of a quite straightforward kind. But this is in another
sense quite consistent with Hawes's concerns. For his discussion of
rhetoric has stressed the application of rational understanding to perceive the moral truth of poetry, to provide a way of reading poetry that
is not limited to entertainment but understands its didactic exposition.

It would, however, be misleading to see Hawes as simply maintain-
ing that poetry makes people better if they read it carefully enough. For
it is clear that in Hawes's scheme rhetoric and the poet are linked to a
particular form of conduct. It is not just a force for moral good. It has a
particular function within the body politic to create stability and order.
It is, in fact, a form of law and order:

> Before the lawe in a tumblyng barge
> The people sayled without parfytenes
> Throughe the worlde all aboute at large
> They hadde none ordre nor no stedfastnes
> Tyll rethorycyans founde Iustyce doubtles
> Ordenynge kynges of ryghte hye dygnyte
> Of all comyns to haue the souerainte.
>
> (876–82)

It is the poet/rhetorician "who led mankind from the state of nature into
civil society and the rule of law."[21]

It is not surprising to find one of Henry VII's courtier/poets affirming the political value of poetry. As we have seen in chapter 1, Henry
had already established poets within his court for their practical rather
than poetical usefulness. The *Pastime* opens with an address to the king.

And Graunde Amour's quest is placed within a context of political well-being. At the beginning of the poem Fame speaks approvingly of the activities "Of noble men in olde tyme to deuyse / Suche thynges as were to the comyn proffet" (240–41). The term "common profit" is a frequently used one in late medieval literature, usually denoting the general good of the state. Hawes alludes to this notion elsewhere in the early part of his poem when he speaks of the "comyn prouffyte of all humanyte" (542).

He contrasts this situation with that obtaining in his own day:

> But now a dayes the contrary is vsed
> To wynne the money theyr studyes be all sette
> The comyn prouffyte is often refused
> For well is he that maye the money gette
> From his neyghboure without ony lette.
>
> (554–58)

And later, during his discussion of rhetoric, he alludes again to this contemporary pursuit of avarice, linking it to a failure to listen to the lessons of poetry:

> But now of dayes the synne of auaryce
> Exyleth the mynde and the hole delyght
> To coueyt connynge whiche is grete preiudyce
> For insacyatly so blynded is theyr syght . . .
> The olde sawes they ryght clene abiect
> Whiche for our lernynge the poetes dyde wryte.
>
> (1275–78, 1282–83)

The emphasis on the "synne of auaryce" is a remarkably recurrent one, both in the *Pastime* and in other of Hawes's poems, as we will see later in this chapter and in chapter 3. I will return to its broader significance later. For the present what is most relevant is the way in which Hawes ascribes this sin to a failure to heed the lessons of poetry. He spells out clearly the specific role of rhetoric in serving the common good:

> Thus the poetes conclude full closely
> Theyr fruytfull problemes for reformacyon

> To make vs lerne to lyue dyrectly
> Theyr good entent and trewe construccyon
> Shewynge to vs the hole affeccyon
> Of the waye of vertue welthe and stablenes
> And to shyt the gate of myscheuous entres.
>   (1114–20)

The poet becomes, in effect, the exponent of a pragmatic morality, adherence to which brings practical benefits: "vertue, welthe and stablesnes."[22] Hawes clearly saw a direct connection between the importance of poetry and contemporary political events.

This connection is reflected in important aspects of the design of the poem. Rhetoric, and hence the poet and the poem he is creating, become important as ways of demonstrating "common profit." The allegorical structure of the poem is concerned to define and enact the qualities of conduct necessary for the well-being of the ordered governance of the realm. Indeed, as we have already seen, the poem is more concerned with showing the acquisition and articulation of these qualities than with their demonstration in action. Stress falls primarily on the depiction of an *educative* process. Fame observes to Graunde Amour as soon as he has elected to seek to win La Belle Pucelle:

> Ye shall . . . atayne the vyctory
> Yf you wyll do as I shall to you saye
> And all my lesson retayne in memory.
>   (295–97)

We follow Graunde Amour through the process of acquiring the qualities appropriate to his aspirations, especially a knowledge of rhetoric. It is necessary for Graunde Amour to gain the lineaments of intellectual and chivalric education to equip himself, not simply to win La Belle Pucelle, but also to cope with the related responsibilities that go with marriage to a princess—responsibilities, that is, of a ruler. Fame, at the beginning of his quest, invokes the example of history to justify this responsibility imposed upon all who achieve a position of noble authority so to educate themselves:

> O ye estates surmountynge in noblesse
> Remembre well the noble paynyms all
> How by theyr laboure they wanne the hyenesse
> Of worthy fame to reygne memoryall
> *And them applyed euer in specyall*
> *Thynges to practyse whiche shoulde prouffyte be*
> *To the comyn welthe and theyr heyres in fee.*
> (246–52; my italics)

There is, Hawes suggests, a necessary relationship between political
order and the existence of an appropriately educated ruling class.
Graunde Amour's quest seems directed toward emphasizing that fact
and establishing the nature of that appropriate education, as the
unbalanced discussion of the seven liberal arts and the stress of rhetoric
suggests. One may wonder why Hawes felt it necessary to make this
point. The lack of any clear knowledge of Hawes's life and circumstances must make any speculation highly tentative. But his oblique
allusions to irresponsible contemporary poetry and the pursuit of
avarice suggest that his design may have been intended to have a
specific applicability to the court circle of which he was a part. Further
speculation must be postponed until other aspects of the poem have
been examined.

The Quest and the Subversion of Expectation

This appropriate education is not limited to Graunde Amour's study
of the Seven Liberal Arts. He proceeds from there to the Tower of
Chivalry and to an exposition of the requisite chivalric virtues. Once
more the nature of the exposition is given a possible direct contemporary relevance. Graunde Amour is told by the porter at the Tower of
Chivalry that

> Vnto this toure ye must resorte by ryght
> For to renue that hath be longe decayd
> The floure of chyualry.
> (2984–86)

This may imply some dissatisfaction with noble conduct as Hawes perceives it within his own milieu, the world of "real" politics.

Once again, stress is placed on the practical, political significance and function of this aspect of Graunde Amour's education. King Melizius, who seems to represent an ideal of kingly, chivalric excellence, makes this clear:

> Knyghthode he sayd was fyrst establysshed
> The comyn welthe in ryght to defende
> That by the wronge it be no mynysshed
> So euery knyght must truely condyscende
> For the comyn welthe his power to entende.
> (3361–65)

The paramount importance of the preservation of the "comyn welthe" recurs, establishing a degree of continuity with Graunde Armour's earlier education.

His sojourn at the Tower of Chivalry is quite brief and contains no systematic exposition of chivalric values. Most of his time there is spent at the temple of Mars, representative deity in the poem for noble action. There Graunde Amour listens to a dialogue between Mars and Fortune as to their respective degrees of power over the affairs of men. Fortune argues that "la graunde amour / Must sue vnto me to do hym socoure" (3191–92). Mars counters with the view that "The man is fortune in the propre dede / And not thou that causeth hym to spede" (3212–13)—in effect, Fortune is simply a convenient figure for man's own responsibilities to himself.

The discussion seems oddly placed and its relevance to what follows may seem not at all clear, especially since the debate lacks any clear resolution. But its placement may be significant. It raises the question of man's responsibility for his own destiny through his actions at a moment just before Graunde Amour actually begins his quest. And it serves to set that quest in some larger sense of that ultimate destiny in a way that mutedly looks forward to the final, dramatic climax to the poem.

After Graunde Amour leaves King Melizius there is a marked change of direction and tone. The didactic and expository concerns and the tone of oblique political criticism are dropped. Instead, at the beginning of the quest proper the poem begins to explore at some length and with differing techniques the nature of human love. Although love has provided the point of departure for Graunde Amour's quest, it has remained virtually unexplored throughout the first half of the poem, apart from the "dolorous and lowly dysputacyon" between the two lovers which interrupts the visit to the Tower of Doctrine. Although we never quite lose sight of the ultimate purpose of the expository sections in the first part of the poem, it is only afterwards that love becomes a matter of central concern.

But the concern is of an ambiguous kind. The first person Graunde Amour encounters after quitting the Tower of Chivalry is the grotesque dwarf Godfrey Gobelive. With Godfrey we go from a world of abstractions to one of gross particularity. Godfrey is a "folysshe dwarfe" (3489) "cladde in a knaues skynne" (3513), of apelike mien (3498). His appearance is matched by a coarseness of utterance that is emphasized by the metrical differentiation in the forms of his speech from Hawes's usual rhyme royal. He uses couplets to assail Graunde Amour with tales of graceless, faithless women and shows the ways in which they can delude even the most noble and distinguished of men. His main examples are of the follies of Aristotle and Vergil. The former, for love of a woman, permits himself to be saddled and bridled and ridden by her:

> So on the grounde Arystotle crepte
> And in his tethe she longe the brydle kepte
> Tyll she therof had ynough her fyll
> And yet for this he neuer had his wyll
> She dyde nothynge but for to mocke and scorne.
> (3614–18)

Vergil is publicly held up to ridicule and scorn when he consented to be raised, at night, in a basket to his lover's chamber. She, however, left him suspended in mid-air, where he remained exposed to public ridicule. His crude revenge is described in detail. Employing his "magykes art" Vergil[23]

> at her buttockes set a brennynge cole
> No fyre there was but at her ars hole
> She torned her tout that was cryspe and fat
> All about Rome dyde fetche theyr fyre therat.
>   (3716–19)

Godfrey is part of a lengthy tradition of antifeminist writings.[24] He is conscious of this and justifies his coarse narratives on the ground of their exemplary function:

> All this I tell though that I be a fole
> To the yonge knyght for thou mayst go to scole
> In tyme comynge of true loue to lerne
> Beware of that for thou canst not decerne
> Thy ladyes mynde though that she speke the fayre
> Her herte is false she wyll no trouthe repayre.
>   (3730–35)

It is hard to know what to make of this episode. The applicability of Godfrey's tales and antifeminist stance to the events of the main narrative is obscure. La Belle Pucelle is not unfaithful to Graunde Amour, nor do Godfrey's words affect his attitude toward her. The whole passage strikes a discordant and seemingly inconsequential note, impeding once again the forward movement of the narrative for no readily apparent purpose.

Godfrey subsequently reappears to be punished and seemingly repudiated for his attitude to women. He rejoins Graunde Amour after the latter's departure from the court of Venus. He is pursued by Dame Correction, who characterizes him as "false report," binds him, and carries him off to the Tower of Correction. The tower affords further elaboration of this preoccupation with faithless lovers as Dame Correction shows Graunde Amour the various levels of her dungeons in which are sequestered various categories of the unfaithful (4112–4269). In this passage Hawes again abandons rhyme royal for couplets.

Once again, the episode raises an issue which is not an issue in the plot of the poem—Graunde Amour's constancy in his pursuit of La Belle Pucelle is never in question; Dame Correction herself terms him "the perfyte floure / Of all true louers" (4141–42). The function of

Godfrey Gobelive and the two couplet passages associated with his appearance is perplexing in the extreme in its seeming stylistic and thematic discord with what has preceded. If one is not simply to dismiss it as gratuitous ineptitude, how is it to be justified?

I believe that its function is akin to that of the earlier dialogue between Mars and Fortune which Graunde Amour overhears, and which seems equally odd (although for different reasons) in its context. Here we find the poem raising some hitherto unexplored questions about the nature of human love with which Graunde Amour's quest is concerned. The existence of unfaithful, unhappy, and dishonorable lovers is established so as to provide a perspective on Graunde Amour's pursuit of La Belle Pucelle. It does not so much suggest their love is like this as remind us of the imperfections to which earthly love can fall prey. It raises for the first time a consciousness of love as not necessarily tending toward a happy outcome. It provides a further intimation that the end of Graunde Amour's quest is not the end of his experience and that what he has learned is not the whole true sum of that experience. For all his gross discordancy Godfrey Gobelive offers a counterstatement to the poem's main strand of exposition that is ultimately to become complementary, not contrary, to it.

Even within the main narrative movement of the poem there emerge muted ambiguities in the presentation of love. Sandwiched between his two encounters with Godfrey Gobelive is Graunde Amour's visit to the Court of Venus. While he is there Venus writes a letter on his behalf to La Belle Pucelle. The argument of the letter is curious in the way its emphases contrast with Graunde Amour's own emphasis on the moral excellence of his beloved as one who is "gentyll good vertuous" (3875) and "whiche all vertues hath so vndefyled" (3880). Venus's letter ignores such moral considerations and instead articulates a highly pragmatic view of human relationships and love. Venus's letter begins by enunciating a *carpe diem* argument:

> Consyder well that your lusty courage
> Age of his cours must at the last transporte
> Now trouth of ryght dooth our selfe exorte
> That you your youth in ydlenes wyll spende
> Withouten pleasure to brynge it to an ende.
> (3953–57)

Or again:

> What you auayleth your beaute so fayre
> Your lusty youthe and gentyll countenaunce
> Without that you in your mynde wyll repayre
> It for to spend in Ioye and pleasaunce.
>
> (3986–89)

Venus stresses the need to seize the ephemeral joys of sensuality before youth and beauty decay. La Belle Pucelle is reminded that "to loue vnloued . . . it is no game" (4046). Emphasis is laid on the importance of "pleasure," a word that echoes through Venus's letter (e.g., 3957, 3968, 4013, 4020, and also its related form "pleasaunce," 3989, 4024). Resistance to the promptings of "lusty youthe" (3987) is, Venus argues, a flouting of the intentions and purposes of Nature

> Than of dame nature what is the entent
> But for to accomplysshe her fayre sede to sowe
> In suche a place as is conuenyent
> To goddes pleasure for to encrease and growe
> The kynde of her ye may not ouerthrowe.
>
> (3965–69)

In this, as in other aspects of this passage, it is hard to avoid the suspicion of irony. Traditionally in medieval literature it is Venus who is subordinate to Nature; the latter is presented as the embodiment of reason and order.[25] Here Nature is presented as an extension of the "pleasure" identified with Venus. The pursuit of this pleasure is made all the more urgent by the passing of time. The terms of the argument—time and pleasure—recall in an oblique and punning way the title of Hawes's poem. Such a recollection adds further to the irony. For this episode seems to undercut, like the Godfrey Gobelive episodes, the elevated abstractions of the initial educative phase of the quest. It reminds us of realities that are both cruder and inexorable, human folly and the constant passage of time. Placed as they are between the movement from education into action, these episodes serve a pivotal function to which I will return.

After his second encounter with Godfrey Gobelive and his visit to Dame Correction, Graunde Amour faces the first test of his martial prowess. He meets the three-headed monster representing the threats to love of falsehood, imagination, and perjury. He is then cheered to receive La Belle Pucelle's response to the letter Venus has sent on his behalf. She professes her love for him and also sends a "goodly shelde" (4635) to protect him. With its aid he defeats the seven-headed monster, whose heads represent dissimulation, delay, discomfort, variance, envy, detraction, and duplicity. Finally, before entering La Belle Pucelle's castle, he has to destroy the seven-metaled monster named "malyce preuy" (5111), the creation of "dame straugenes" and "dame dysdayne" (4949). He is then ready to claim La Belle Pucelle in marriage.

This summary may give an impression of rapidity or urgency of movement as we enter a section of the poem ostensibly concerned with the narrative of action. If so, the impression is misleading. These three episodes are covered in less than a thousand lines (4270–5186). And it is difficult to avoid the impression that Hawes is anxious to deal with them as briefly as possible. As nearly as I can calculate, the actual accounts of Graunde Amour's battles are perfunctory in the extreme, occupying fewer than 150 lines within the three episodes.[26] More stress is given to the description of the actual monsters and to an account of the processes whereby La Belle Pucelle granted him her love (4522–4640) than to actual narration.

One is tempted to see this whole section as a flaw in the poem's design. Having seen Graunde Amour so extensively prepared to be a chivalrous knight, we see precious little of him in action. But such a view is, of course, predicated on an assumption that human action, however potentially heroic, is any real part of Hawes's concern. In fact, Hawes seems more interested in what Graunde Amour confronts than the way he confronts it. We see him triumphing over a series of moral and spiritual impediments. We see several demonstrations of the efficacy of Graunde Amour's education. The poem seems to suggest that such a man, steeped in virtuous education, should have relatively little difficulty in overcoming such adversities. It is the *consequences* of the triumph of virtue that prove of greater moment and, in effect, validate Hawes's refusal to place much narrative weight on the exploration of heroic narrative.

Death and Judgment

The reasons for this refusal become clearer in the concluding sections of the *Pastime*. The movement to a new mode of presentation is signaled by the abrupt disappearance from the poem of La Belle Pucelle, hitherto the ostensible focus of all Graunde Amour's endeavors. Immediately after his marriage to her she ceases to have any significant role: "Thus with my lady that was fayre and clere / In Ioye I lyued full ryght many a yere" (5332–33) is all that is said about her.

Instead, the poem moves swiftly from their wedding, the moment of supreme happiness, to the very end of Graunde Amour's life, when age and death "arrest" him. At this moment Graunde Amour presents himself to the audience not as the youthful questing hero; as he says "My youthe was paste and all my lustynes" (5370). Instead, he presents himself as insensately preoccupied with the acquisition of wealth:

> My hole pleasure and delyte doubtles
> Was sette vpon treasure insacyate
> It to beholde and for to agregate . . .
> This was my mynde and all my purueyaunce
> As vpon dethe I thought lytell or neuer
> But gadred ryches as I sholde lyue euer.
> (5373–75, 5380–82)

The terms of this self-accusation recall the earlier argument of Venus who argued for pleasure because of the passage of time, and who seems to be ironically undercut. It also recalls the earliest preoccupation with the harmful pursuit of wealth, the "sin of avarice" to which Hawes alludes during Graunde Amour's visit to the Tower of Doctrine. And there is once again the punning reiteration of the poem's title ("My youthe was *past* . . . My hole *pleasure* . . . was sett"). In such ways do we see the conclusion of the *Pastime* seeking to begin to draw together seemingly diverse strands of its previous concerns.

In this conclusion Hawes achieves his most powerful tonal effect. After Graunde Amour has been shriven and his body buried "full ryght humbly" (5412), there appear before him in his grave in a pageantlike series of sequences, the Seven Deadly Sins, the Nine Worthies, Fame, Time, and Eternity. The ultimate source of these sequences is undoubtedly Petrarch's *Trionfi,* which depicts in turn the triumph of Chastity over Love, Death over Chastity, Fame over Death, Time over Fame, and the final triumph of Eternity. But Hawes's source is less likely to have been Petrarch's actual text than some visual representation of it.[27]

The sequence opens with the Seven Deadly Sins, the subject of an extensive medieval tradition.[28] The sins are linked in their presentation through the iterative use of the phrase "erthe upon erthe." Considerable play is made upon this phrase, which is the opening one of one of the most popular Middle English didactic lyrics, "variants of which are actually found on English tombstones."[29] In Graunde Amour's case, too, "ouer my graue to be in memory / Remembraunce made this lytell epytaphy" (5416–17). The particular example of Graunde Amour then becomes generalized into a homiletic verity:

> And my selfe called la graunde amoure
> Sekynge aduenture in the worldly glory
> For to attayne the ryches and honoure
> Dyde thynke full lytell that I sholde here ly
> Tyll dethe dyde marke me full ryght pryuely
> Lo what I am and where to you must
> Lyke as I am so shall you be all dust.
>
> (5481–87)

To this extent the poem is unambiguously medieval in its orientation. It offers a dramatic affirmation of the inexorable realities of mutability and sin in human affairs, leading to the ultimate reality of death for those who set their minds on "worldly glory."

But the poem does not end there. The didactic orthodoxy of this sequence is followed by the reappearance of Fame, Graunde Amour's original guide at the beginning of *Pastime.* She is surrounded, as she was then, by "brennynge tongues" (5497), and seeks to offer a counterstatement to the preceding assertions of the mutability of human endeavors. "For though his body be deed and mortall / His fame shall dure and be memoryall," she claims (5507–8). She goes on to maintain that "I shall his name so dryue / That euermore without extyngys-shemente / In brennynge tongues he shall be parmanente" (5520–22). The achievements of Graunde Amour become linked to those of the Nine Worthies—Hector, Joshua, Judas Maccabeus, David, Alexander,

Julius Caesar, Arthur, Charlemagne, and Godfrey of Boulogne. The Nine Worthies were another medieval commonplace with an extensive tradition[30] of exemplary knightly prowess. Here it is juxtaposed against the earlier "erthe upon erthe" motif, to affirm the enduring nature of fame:

> And thus I fame am euer magnyfyed
> Whan erth in erthe hath tane his estate
> Thus after dethe I am all gloryfyed
> What is he nowe that can my power abate
> Infenyte I am nothynge can me mate.
>   (5600–5604)

But this affirmation is followed in its turn by a still further one: the appearance of the figure of Time, affirming anew the mutability of human affairs:

> I meruayle moche of the presumpcyon
> Of the dame fame so puttynge in vre
> Thy grete prayse saynge it shall endure
> For to be infynyte euermore in preace
> Seynge that I shall all thy honor seace.
>   (5630–34)

Time maintains its presence as the subsuming force in worldly matters: "Withouten tyme is no erthely thynge" (5677). He is subordinate only to "dame eternyte," who concludes the pageant of figures.

Dame Eternity also stresses human mutability: "worldly Ioye and frayle prosperyte / What is it lyke but a blast of wynde?" she asks (5776–77). It is to preparation for a life outside time, and hence exempt from corruption, that man should direct himself:

> Whan erthe in erth hath tane his corrupte taste
> Than to repente it is for you to late
> Whan you haue tyme spende it nothynge in waste
> Tyme past with vertue must entre the gate
> Of Ioye and blysse with myn hye estate
> Withouten tyme for to be euerlastynge
> Whiche god graunte vs at our last endynge.
>   (5781–88)

Here the poem ends. Only a brief prayer to the Virgin Mary and a formal *envoi* follow. C. S. Lewis has praised the ending of the *Pastime* as "one of the most nobly conceived passages in any allegory,"[31] even if execution does not necessarily match conception.[32] Certainly Hawes shows an inclination to enlarge the range of his concerns in this section, moving away from either of the dominant modes of the earlier parts of his poem, didactic allegory or chivalric romance. In this final section Hawes adopts more impersonal and iconographically dramatic techniques.

Some Principles of Unity

Such a chronological discussion of the various episodes of the *Pastime* and the difficulties they pose may be felt to evade the problem with which we began: the sense in the poem of a confusing heterogeneity, bereft of any clear focus. Do the various episodes of the poem cohere around some controlling concern or concerns which can be said to establish a unifying principle?

One might begin with the title—*The Pastime of Pleasure*. To the best of my knowledge no one has attempted to establish what this title is intended to signify. And yet Hawes does give some emphasis to its terms in the course of his poem. "Pleasure" is an often-used word. For example, places at which Graunde Amour stops are often "place[s] of pleasure,"[33] culminating in the description of the "chambre fayre / A place of pleasure and delectacyon" (5243–44) where he is finally united with La Belle Pucelle. And after their marriage we are told that he "lyued in such pleasure gladde" (5348) until he is enjoined to "forsake pleasure and to lerne to dy" (5424).

"Pastime" is more difficult to define. The word is never used in the poem. It seems to be used in a sense no longer current, of "an interval between two points of time."[34] For what the *Pastime of Pleasure* chronicles is a sequence of events from Graunde Amour's choice of the Active Life until his death; that is, the finite limit of his "pleasure" within the world. As we have already seen, the concluding section of the poem, after Graunde Amour's death, begins with play upon the two components of the title. For it is at this point it is possible to perceive the limited temporal and moral perspectives that Graunde Amour has permitted to define and dominate his pursuit of the Active Life.

In retrospect it is relatively easy to see that the final vision of death, time, and eternity only makes explicit a moral vision that has been implicit from the moment Graunde Amour chose the Active Life. The way of life he rejected was the "streyght waye of contemplacyon" (85) with its promise of ultimate well-being at the "Ioyfull toure perdurable" (86). He is told that

> Who that wyll walke vnto that mancyon
> He must forsake all thynges varyable
> With the vayneglory somoche deceyuable
> And thoughe the waye be harde and daungerous
> The laste ende therof shall be ryght precyous.
>
> (87–91)

In contrast the only promise the Active Life offers is the winning of "La Belle Pucelle." In effect, Graunde Amour, in choosing the Active Life, is choosing to submit himself to the inevitable mutable process of time rather than the "toure perdurable."

This commitment to a choice that holds only the promise of ephemeral rewards is consistently implied when Graunde Amour begins to undertake the Active Life, i.e., after he leaves the Tower of Doctrine. We have already seen the instances of this: the stress of human responsibility at the Tower of Chivalry; the gross ridicule of women by Godfrey Gobelive; the highly equivocal portrayal of Venus; the refusal of the poem to interest itself in Graunde Amour's heroic achievements. All these episodes provide contexts of pessimism for any evaluation of Graunde Amour's choice, a pessimism that culminates with the abrupt disappearance of La Belle Pucelle from the poem after her lover's final victory. These episodes all prepare the way for Hawes's final overtly didactic vision of human mutability. In this final vision we see the ultimate consequences of Graunde Amour's initial choice of the Active Life, a choice made through a rational exercise of free will. In the end Time's eroding power makes all his achievements and pleasure "past." We are left to contemplate the immutable verity of Eternity with its admonition.

> O mortall folke reuolue in your mynde
> That worldly Ioye and frayle prosperyte
> What is it lyke but a blaste of wynde

> For you therof can haue no certaynte
> It is now so full of mutabylyte
> Set not your mynde vpon wordly welthe
> But euermore regarde your soules helthe.
>
> (5775–81)

It is possible to perceive, then, a rejection of the values of the Active Life consistently woven into the design of Graunde Amour's quest. But how does this rejection relate to the first half of the poem, to the visit to the Tower of Doctrine with its stress on the practical educative benefits of poetry.

We saw there the function of poetry defined as primarily moral. The poet imposes order on society through telling the truth in a form that society could understand, through allegorical "fables." But this is contrasted with the situation Hawes sees existing "now a dayes" where people are concerned less with learning to pursue the "common profit" and to study literature with such an end in view. Instead, poetry is devoted to "makynge balades of feruent amyte" (1391) and mankind is shown as devoted to the "synne of auaryce" (1275). It is worth recalling that avarice and a failure to heed the lessons of poetry are both seen as symptoms of contemporary malaise. Graunde Amour's education and quest can be reasonably seen as Hawes's attempt to reflect this malaise, as the narrative of a man capable of heroic conduct but whose actions are undercut and finally vitiated by his failure to learn the lessons of poetry and support the "common profit," pursuing instead insensate covetousness and engaging in a quest that proves ultimately of negligible value and significance.

Hence it is incorrect to consider the poem as leading at its climax to a "surprising shift from romance to allegory."[35] I would prefer to suggest that the concerns of romance are consistently subverted and the allegorical concerns consistently developed. Graunde Amour's emphasis on wealth is not one that suddenly emerges at the conclusion of the poem. Before he first meets La Belle Pucelle he protests to Counsel that

> Alas quod I she is of hye degre
> Borne to grete londe treasure and substaunce
> I fere to fore I shall dysdayned be
> The whiche wyll trouble all my greuaunce
> Her beaute is the cause of my penaunce

> I haue no grete lande treasure and ryches
> To wynne the fauoure of her noblenesse.
>
> (1849–55)

He stresses their relative disparity in wealth. Counsel responds:

> What thoughe quod he drawe you not abacke
> For she hath ynoughe in her possessyon
> For you both for you shall neuer lacke
> Yf that ye ordre it by good reason.
>
> (1856–59)

Counsel offers the notion of sufficiency rather than wealth ("she hath ynoughe . . . for you both") provided that Graunde Amour will be constrained by "good reason." Interestingly, Venus uses substantially the same argument in her letter to La Belle Pucelle, denying any importance to lack of "lande or substaunce":

> Where that is loue there can be no lacke
> Fye on that loue for the lande or substaunce
> For it must nedes ryght soone abacke
> Whan that youth hath no Ioy nor pleasaunce
> In the party with natures suffycysaunce
> That wyll you for the *synne of aueryche*
> Vnto your youth do such a preiudyce.
>
> (4021–27; my italics)

But in spite of these and other warnings at the Tower of Doctrine, Graunde Amour does succumb to the "sin of avarice." And while the sudden revelation of his fault may be abrupt, it is not arbitrary but grows out of a recurrently enunciated concern in the *Pastime*.

This does not, of course, answer the underlying question: *why* was Hawes so preoccupied with the "sin of avarice"? Why does he place so much stress on it in his poem? It is not possible to answer the question with certainty. Legitimate speculation may, however, point toward a possible solution.

We know that Hawes was a member of Henry VII's Privy Chamber, and, as such, in a position to observe intimately the character of the king and the formulation of royal policies during the last part of Henry's reign. The *Pastime* opens with an appropriately deferential address to the king (1–56) which concludes with a rather defensive passage:

> For vnder a colour a truthe maye aryse
> As was the guyse in olde antyquyte
> Of the poetes olde a tale to surmyse
> To cloke the trouthe of theyr infyrmyte
> Or yet on Ioye to haue moralyte
> I me excuse yf by neclygence
> That I do offende for lacke of scyence.
> (50–56)

In part this passage is a defense of allegorical poetry, a defense we have discussed earlier. But there is a muffled insistence on revealing "truth" (50, 53). The modesty *topos* is too formulaically conventional to afford much basis for conclusion, but it is worth asking what "truth" might Hawes feel it appropriate to represent allegorically that might run the risk of offending Henry in a poem written around 1505/6.

A possible answer can be found in some lines in Hawes's later poem, *A Joyful Meditation,* which celebrates the accession of Henry VIII. There he speaks of his former master

> Our late souerayne his fader excellent
> I knowe ryght well some holde oppynyon
> That to auaryce he had entendement
> Gadrynge grete rychesse of this his regyon.
> (71–74)

This contemporary manifestation of the "sin of avarice" requires a little explanation of the history of Henry's reign. After his victory at Bosworth Field in 1485 Henry's chief concern was to establish the central power of the monarchy against the contending forces of individual noble factions. The main means he chose were attainder and financial sanctions. Both had the effect of depriving the nobility of the wealth which confirmed their status. When peers were permanently attainted, their property automatically reverted to the Crown. When Henry permitted the reversal of attainder it was on payment of fines.[36]

In the latter part of his reign, from 1502 onward, Henry's financial policies became more wide ranging and more rapacious. As Polydore Vergil notes in his *Historia Anglicana* for that year: "Thus the good prince [Henry] by degrees lost all sense of moderation and was led into avarice."[37] He developed elaborate systems of bonds and recognizances which were in effect little more than arbitrary levies of money, not restricted to the nobility, and enforced through his ministers Empson and Dudley—to whom Hawes alludes in *A Joyful Meditation* (see chap. 3). Hawes was not alone in commenting after Henry's death on the avariciousness of his later years. But it is unsurprising that, if he wished to express his concerns on the matter while the king was alive, he should have chosen the obliquity of allegory.

We follow a noble protagonist "descended of the gentyll lyne" (4008) through education, achievement, and marriage to his final pursuit of "treasure insacyate" (5374). The potential contemporary applicability for Hawes's audience would be clear. This is not to suggest that the poem is simply a clumsy topical allegory distended to tedious length. In a more general way, as we have seen, Hawes expresses pessimism at all manifestations of the Active Life, steadily undercutting the progress of his hero in various ways. He also asserts a concern for political responsibility, the "common profit" which while it may have a specific applicability is also concerned with providing a justification for the poet's function—and, indeed, for the poem he has written. The *Pastime of Pleasure* is a more structurally coherent poem than has been generally perceived once one grasps the underlying purposes that control the apparently random jumble of its components.

The Failure of Style

The problem with this poem is that Hawes's technical resources are not equal to his conception. A major difficulty is his uncertain grasp of meter, which has been most temperately described as "broken backed"[38] and often as much worse.[39] The lines are highly irregular, ranging from eight to twelve syllables and from four to six stresses.[40] While, as I will suggest in chapter 4, such criticism is rather unfair, Hawes seems to have a limited sense of aural effects, of the possible relationship between sound and sense in his verse. Apart from some fine sonorous passages in the conclusion of the *Pastime,* the best effect he can achieve is the clashing contrast of the couplet passages in the Godfrey Gobelive episodes.

Nor does his diction have the power much of the time to reflect experience or narrative in other than the most banal terms. As his editor ruefully observes, "he was too likely to smother his thoughts, to say nothing of his poetry, under a blanket of pedantic verbiage," expressing himself in language that is "flatly prosaic."[41] To this must be added a poverty of invention that results in repeated use of the same collocations and even the same lines on numerous occasions.[42] In addition, a considerable number of lines are borrowed outright or with only minor alterations from his earlier *Example of Virtue*.[43] There is abundant evidence of impoverished poetic ingenuity.

It is such stylistic failures that weaken the *Pastime of Pleasure*.[44] The crucial limiting factor in our response to his verse is this general inability to realize in it attitudes or emotions other than at the level of banality. One sees this clearly in the most famous stanza of the *Pastime,* which comes near the end:

> O mortall folke you may beholde and se
> How I lye here somtyme a myghty knyght
> The ende of Ioye and all prosperyte
> Is dethe at last through his course and myght
> After the day there cometh the derke nyght
> For though the day be neuer so longe
> At last the belles ryngeth to euensonge.
>   (5474–80)

What we see here is the way in which Hawes's attempts to achieve any kind of dramatic realization slide immediately into proverbial triteness. In fact the stanza, including the often-quoted final couplet, is a tissue of proverbial commonplaces,[45] drawn together to give a texture of sentious utterance. Derek Pearsall is right to criticize Hawes as "a poet whose ambitions far outrun his capacity."[46]

But the *Pastime of Pleasure* remains a genuine literary achievement, albeit of a flawed kind. We see Hawes struggling to find appropriate form to express complex concerns. He tries to articulate a vision of human affairs that attempts to encompass the temporal and the timeless, the secular and the moral, and to discharge conscientiously his sense of his own poetic responsibilities even though doing so might result in some personal risk or adversity. His shaping of his materials may often seem cumbersome, his execution at times inept. But his efforts are more successful than has often been realized. The *Pastime* does have a structural coherence and intermittent but genuine poetic force that merit much more appreciation than the poem generally receives.

Chapter Three
The Minor Poems

The Example of Virtue

The Example of Virtue is Hawes's first recorded poem. De Worde's 1509 edition describes it as written "by Stephyn hawys one of the gromes of our souereyne lorde kynge Henry the .vii. the .xix. yere of his moost nobell reygne and by hym presented to our sayd souerayne lorde." This would date the poem's composition 1503/4 and may imply that it was presented in manuscript form to the king at that time. There is no clear reason for the delay between composition and de Worde's printing.

The Example of Virtue is the second longest of Hawes's works. It consists of 2,129 lines, all in rhyme royal except for a single stanza (1394–1401). The plot can be swiftly summarized. During September, the narrator has a dream in which he is summoned by Morpheus, who takes him to meet a beautiful lady, Discretion. She gives him a series of injunctions or "prouerbes" (121) and then takes him on a ship named *Vainglory.* Together they sail to an island ruled by four ladies—Nature, Fortune, Hardiness, and Wisdom. The dreamer and his guide visit their dwellings in turn before listening to a debate among the four before Dame Justice. Each of the four argues before Justice that she is the most profitable to man. Justice concludes, however, that they should be "copertyners" (1035)′ in guiding the welfare of man. The other four all agree to her conclusion.

After the debate, the dreamer, now named Youth and later to be designated Virtue, is told by Dame Sapience of "a lady of meruelous beaute" (1058). He sets out to seek her, accompanied by Discretion. On his journey he encounters various temptations—Sensuality, Pride, and Worldly Fashion—before reaching the dwelling of the lady, called Cleanness, and her father, the King of Love. Here Virtue dons the Pauline armor of righteousness and slays a three-headed dragon. He weds Cleanness in an elaborate ceremony.

59

The poem then moves abruptly from the marriage ceremony to the death of the protagonist. At his death he is granted a vision of the depths of hell before ascending to the joys of heaven. The *Example* concludes with prayers to Henry VII, his mother, Margaret Beaufort, and his son, the future Henry VIII.

As such a summary suggests there are obvious parallels between this poem and the later *Pastime of Pleasure.* Both are cast in the form of allegorical quests directed toward the revelation of some form of moral truth. Both sandwich episodes of knightly prowess between passages of static exposition. Both follow the fortunes of a young protagonist toward triumphs in valor and in love and follow him beyond these to death. And in both this protagonist is student and knight attempting to make manifest in his deeds what he has learned. Such parallels are strengthened, in a more local way, by the frequent self-borrowing to which Hawes resorts in the later *Pastime,* transferring phrases, lines, and even stanzas into it from the *Example.*

To a greater degree than was the case in the *Pastime of Pleasure,* the generic model of the *Example of Virtue* appears to be the Pilgrimage of Life. I have discussed the general features of this genre in the previous chapter and will not repeat them here. It may, however, be worth pointing out that in some respects this earlier poem shows a more direct commitment to the implications of this genre than the later work. For example, it uses the dream vision convention and it makes a more compressed attempt to focus centrally on the problems of man's spiritual health and well-being, eschewing the sometimes egregious digressions of the later work, such as the Godfrey Gobelive episodes.[1]

A few other generic models may have had some influence on the poem. The argument before Dame Justice recalls the form of the numerous Middle English debate poems, although the nature and precise form of the debate appear unique.[2] A similar very general indebtedness to the genre of visions of heaven and hell can be found in its concluding section.[3]

It is probable that Hawes was influenced by specific works at some points in the *Example.* A few lines are clearly drawn from a late Middle English allegorical dream vision, the *Assembly of Ladies,* and other lines may be.[4] Like *The Example,* the *Assembly of Ladies* combines personification allegory with the debate and dream vision forms. But the verbal parallels are intermittent, and in style and tone the earlier poem is very removed from Hawes's own.

A more extensive influence on the *Example* is the *Court of Sapience,* which is, as we have seen, also a possible source for the *Pastime of Pleasure.* A number of parallels between it and the *Example* have been noted, albeit of a very general kind, but cumulatively they do possess a certain weight of probability.[5] And Hawes's likely use of the *Court of Sapience* may be strengthened by his explicit allusion to another work, the medieval encyclopedia of Bartholomaeus Anglicus, *De Proprietatibus Rerum.* Dame Nature urges her audience "loke in the boke of barthelmewe / And to his scripture take gode hede" (1003–4). De Worde had printed an edition in 1495 in Trevisa's English translation. And the *Court of Sapience* also draws explicitly on Bartholomaeus, particularly in its section on jewels. It may well be that at least some of the lapidary allusions in the *Example*[6] derive indirectly from Bartholomaeus Anglicus through the *Court of Sapience.* Certainly both works are of a didactic and encyclopedic cast that would have appealed to Hawes's taste.

But neither generic analogues nor local sources provide much help in the interpretation of Hawes's poem. The difficulties in responding to it are similar to the problems of response posed by the *Pastime of Pleasure.* We note once again the shifting nature of the form of the poem as it moves from dream vision to debate to quest and transcendental climax, with very few efforts to link these different sections or any attempt to make it adhere overall to the constraints of a particular genre. Thus the dream vision with which the poem opens is never explicitly abandoned but soon ceases to have any relevance to its structure or design. Narrative is abruptly telescoped near the end when the final visionary sequences follow immediately upon the conclusion of Virtue's marriage to Cleanness. The components of the narrative seem sufficiently inexpertly ordered to suggest an apprentice hand at work.

Similar uncertainties seem to surround the actual allegorical technique of the *Example of Virtue.* The lengthy debate among Fortune, Nature, Sapience, and Hardiness seems to bear no specific relationship to the quest that Virtue subsequently undertakes. The allegory of the quest seems inert and perfunctory. When Virtue encounters such figures as Sensuality or Avarice they remain simply people he meets, whose allegorical significance is subsequently expounded to him by Sapience but not in any way enacted or dramatized through the encounter. Stress falls, as elsewhere, on the static visual qualities associated with the figures and their accompanying woodcuts.

At other points it is the allegory itself that is unconvincing. The father of Dame Cleanness, the King of Love, is evidently intended to be a figure of complex allegorical significance—judging by the length and detail of his description (1297–1344)—and one of some Christian importance in the scheme of the poem. But he remains a pagan figure, a "celestial Cupid"[7] whose various attributes are quite arbitrarily designated; for example,

> His one legge is armed to defende
> The ryght that longeth vnto amyte
> And wrong loue for to amende
> His naked legge betokeneth charyte
> That is the Ioye of grete felycyte,
>   (1338–42)

and so on. There is no attempt to show what these attributes mean or how they are expressed in any dynamic way. They are simply asserted and lack any necessary or plausible connection as Christian qualities with the pagan figure to whom they are applied.

Elsewhere allegory is completely abandoned, as in the ending of the poem which is visionary but completely literal in its accounts of the levels of Hell and the joys of Heaven. Throughout there seems a degree of uncertainty as to the function of allegory. Given such uncertainty it is not surprising that Hawes is not really capable of contriving a structure to sustain it adequately.

These are large difficulties and they seriously inhibit any response to the *Example of Virtue*. One might reasonably ask why Hawes elected to employ a mode and form over which his control was so uncertain. Part of the answer may lie in simple inexperience, or limited ability. But another part may lie in what Hawes seems to be trying to say in his poem. It seems possible that he was seeking indirectly and unsuccessfully to express views and feelings that he felt it inappropriate, for whatever reasons, to enunciate clearly. To clarify this assertion it is necessary to ask the basic question: what is the *Example of Virtue* intended to be about?

One might appropriately begin with the apparent implications of plot and title: to see it as an attempt, however flawed in execution, to present a pattern for a virtuous life. At the beginning, Discretion promises Virtue to "brynge thy soule to blesse eterne / By wyse example and morall doctryne" (82–83). It is not, however, always easy to see the poem in terms of this promise, although the general shape of Virtue's activities appears to reflect it. He is exposed to a certain amount of example and doctrine and is brought to eternal bliss. But along the way there is a certain amount of material of a very different kind woven into the poem's fabric. Often it seems to have a texture of apparently contemporary, obliquely political allusion that seems to move the poem's concerns at times away from the timeless significances of moral allegory into the "real" world of Hawes's audience.

The character and composition of this audience merit a little speculation. All the indications are that Hawes saw his poem as addressed directly to the courtly circle of which he was a part. The allusions at the end of it to Henry VII, Margaret Beaufort, and the future Henry VIII are an obvious point here. But there are others which are both more cryptic and more striking.

For example, early in the poem, when Virtue and Discretion meet Dame Sapience, Sapience gives the young man a series of exhortations (372–99) before concluding:

> Now I amytte you into your rome
> In the whiche ye shall your selfe apply
> Of myne owne chaumbre ye shall be grome.
> (400–402)

It is at least a striking coincidence that Virtue should be given the same position, groom of the chamber, that Hawes himself had to Henry VII.

There are other indications of Hawes's apparent consciousness of a direct relationship between what is said in the *Example* and contemporary reality. Dame Hardiness slips into her justification of her own importance, a passage on the factors which create a strong kingdom (610–30). "A realme is vpholden by thynges three" (610), she says. The first is the sword; the second, law; and the third

> . . . be marchauntes that do multyply
> In this realme welth and prosperyte
> For of euery thynge they often occupy
> Euery man lyke vnto his faculte

> For without marchauntes can not be
> No realme vpholden in welth & pleasure
> For it to vs is a specyall tresure.
>
> (624–30)

This has, of course, nothing to do with the attributes of Hardiness, as the reference to "this realme" confirms. Hawes deliberately introduces an anomalous passage into the poem. It is tempting to see here an occasional point being made. For in 1504 (within the period of the composition of the *Example*) Henry did introduce an Act of Parliament giving preferential treatment to merchants of the Hanseatic League over British merchants.[8]

Such occasional preoccupations appear reflected in the design of the first major division of the *Example,* the presentation of and debate among Fortune, Hardiness, Nature, and Sapience. The initial descriptions of these four are strangely unbalanced. Fortune, Hardiness, and Nature are described in 28, 41, and 28 lines, respectively. Sapience is presented in 182, almost twice as many as for the other three. Moreover, Sapience is the only figure of the four who is presented as unequivocally admirable; she is described as

> . . . so fayre and clerely puryfyed
> And so dyscrete and full of womanhede
> That and I trowe vertue were deed
> It sholde reuyue yet in her agayne
> She was so gentyll and without dysdeyn.
>
> (353–57)

The others are all presented in some way which stresses their limitations. Thus Fortune is "fals and full of doblenes" (271). Hardiness is limited by death which "dyde surrendre / And all theyr strength and lusty corage / For he spareth nother youth ne age" (320–22). And Nature is similarly constrained by the reality of Death:

> Me thought she was of merueylous beaute
> Tyll that Dyscrecyon lede me behynde
> Where that I saw all the pryuyte

Of her werke and humayne kynde
And at her backe I dyd than fynde
Of cruell deth a dolfull ymage
That all her beaute dyd perswage.

(519–25)

In addition Sapience (or "dame Prudence" as she is also known) is the only one of the four who speaks in the course of her initial description. She gives Virtue an extended verse sermon, concluding with a lengthy passage of anaphora (463–90).

A similar weighting of the scales in favor of Sapience is again evident during the actual debate before Dame Justice. Once more, quantitative evidence is revealing. The debate covers lines 582–1022. Of the various speakers, Hardiness is given 102 lines; Fortune and Nature, 56 each; and Sapience, 203. Hawes seems clearly concerned to establish a hierarchy of significance among the debaters in which the position of Sapience commands the greatest attention.

The ordering of the debate itself confirms this. As the relative apportioning of lines might suggest, the central discussion is between Hardiness and Sapience. Dame Hardiness begins by claiming that "she was to man moost profytable / For she the hertes hath often fede / Of conqueroures . . ." (583–85). She provides a number of illustrations in support of her claim, drawn from the Nine Worthies and the example of Hercules.

In her response, Sapience seems once again to add to the contemporary political coloring of the poem. She claims that she is "of the kynges counsayll" (869) in responding to Hardiness's arguments. She criticizes such arguments on the grounds that they have harmful implications for the well-being of the state, for "by her foly and folysshe hardynes / She [i.e., Hardiness] causeth men to ryse ayenst theyr lorde" (750–51). This may be an oblique allusion to the various attempts to overthrow Henry VII, notably by Perkin Warbeck, Lambert Simnel, and Rafe Wilford, this last in 1499, less than five years before the composition of the *Example*.

This tendency to disorder on the part of Hardiness is contrasted with Sapience, who appears as the embodiment of Divine Order, who does "procede / Of the strength of the holy ghoost" (813–14). She goes on to

enumerate the six qualities which are characteristic of Sapience: prudence, loyalty, liberality, strength, mercy, and largesse (825–68). The
refrain in this passage describes these as the qualities of a "true crysten
man." But as they are defined they seem to have more relevance to a
system of values more pragmatic in nature and (possibly) more directly
relevant to the situation of Hawes's courtly audience.

For example, loyalty entails that one "sholde be true / To his soue-
rayn lorde . . . / And all treason foreuer to eschewe" (834–36). Liberality means that "he sholde be lyberall / Amonge his commons withouten lette / . . . That he the loue of theym doth gette / For it causeth
theyr hertes on hym to be sette" (841–42, 844–45). And largesse
implies that "a knyght ought for to kepe / The poore folke in theyr
grete nede" (862–63). Clearly the frame of reference for such injunctions has to be a noble audience.

And the orientation of such advice as it is embodied in the presentation of Sapience's characteristics is also clearly social and political. The
explicitly Christian promise of the poem's beginning, to bring Virtue's
soul to "blesse eterne" (82), seems here to be forgotten. The discussion
is rooted firmly in the temporal world of a ruling class. Sapience herself
reminds us of this when she urges that she should "haue the souer-
aynte / As is accordynge to my *royall dygnyte*" (907–8; my italics.)

It seems therefore both plausible and appropriate to see some connection between the concerns enunciated in the debate and the actual
historical milieu in which Hawes wrote it—the court of Henry VII.
And the weight of emphasis clearly falls upon the figure of Sapience and
the qualities of noble comportment with which she is associated. Yet
perhaps the most interesting aspect of the debate lies not in the evident
weight given to her figure and arguments, but rather in the fact she is
not allowed finally to prevail at the conclusion of the debate. For Dame
Justice declines to cast her vote for any of the parties appearing before
her. The implication seems to be that even the qualities of Sapience are
insufficiently transcendent to provide an ultimate example of virtue.

It is after this indeterminate ending that Virtue embarks on his
actual quest. He does so under the guidance of Sapience, who initially
directs him to Cleanness, his future bride, and who reappears to guide
him after he has overcome Sensuality and Covetous Pride, escorting
him to the castle of the King of Love, Cleanness's father, and helping
him overcome the three-headed monster, the World, the Flesh, and the

Devil. Her actions confirm her words, demonstrating her capacity for shrewd and judicious conduct within the world.

But the latter half of the poem is fraught with difficulties. It parallels the movement of the *Pastime of Pleasure* from one of static exposition to a lumbering action which is episodic and disjointed. It crams five distinct episodes into barely a thousand lines: the encounter with temptations, the meeting with the King of Love, the fight with the dragon, the marriage, and the final vision of Heaven and Hell. As this might suggest, not all of these are developed sufficiently for their significance in the overall structure of the poem to be accessible.

Part of the problem lies in the nature of Hawes's allegory. I have already discussed the way it remains flatly literal, lacking a poetic context to give it any dramatic realization. For example, in Virtue's encounter with the temptations, Sensuality and Pride, these figures exist inertly; their encounters are wholly static. Such interest as exists in the episode lies in the way they are interpreted by Sapience. Once again, the representations are seen in courtly, rather than moral, terms. Sensuality is depicted as one who can "well flater with wordes swete" (1193). Pride is depicted as "the synne of auaryce" (1200). They are the embodiments of "worldely fastyon" (1211), viewed in terms which are not the most obvious characteristics of these faults.

This seems to confirm what has already been stressed—the existence of a secular, courtly dimension to Virtue's quest. As before, it is set in very specific worldly terms. This is also the case, to a lesser degree, in the presentation of the King of Love. Once again, the allegory is static and literal. He appears, as has been remarked,[9] as an unreconciled amalgam of attributes. He is blind, naked, and holding a sharp dart, all attributes which seem to identify him as pagan Cupid. But he requires Virtue to overcome Christian representations of evil, "the worlde the flesshe & the deuyll" (1372), donning the Pauline armor of righteousness to do so (1394–1401). The briefly described battle with the three-headed dragon is wholly Christian in the orientation of its allegory.

This movement from secularized to wholly Christian allegorical representations is confirmed in the central episode of the second half of the *Example,* the marriage of Virtue and Cleanness. It is particularly hard to grasp Hawes's intentions here, because of the plethora of historical and allegorical figures who make their appearances. The couple are attended by Moses, St. Augustine, St. Peter, Bede, Gregory, St. Ambrose, and St. Jerome. The guests at the eucharistic meal that follows include St. Edmund and St. Edward. Sundry Virtues, Grace, Humility, Faith, and Contrition, among others, also make appearances. Such a multiplicity of allegorical and historical personages seems seriously to overtax the design of the poem. Every personification that can be linked to virtuous conduct makes a helter-skelter entrance:

> Than went dame reason with perseueraunce
> And than dame mercy with contricyon
> And than exersyce with remembraunce
> After whom went dame restytucyon
> With dame prayer and dame confessyon
> And dame charyte with obedyence
> And after theym came fayre dame abstynence.
>
> (1787–93)

The list goes on, but no one serves any defined function or contributes to any articulated pattern of meaning. Even Sapience, the only allegorical figure who seems to possess any possibility of focusing or ordering the significance of these figures, ends up getting lost in the crowd.

The ending of the poem follows hard on the wedding feast. It makes some attempt to bring together some of the threads of the second part of the poem, as the Angel Raphael shows Virtue the dragon he killed "bounde with chaynes in fyer infynall" (1897) and reflects on the possible consequences if he had chosen to succumb to the temptations of avarice and sensuality (1899–1912). What we see is the apotheosis of the life of virtue within the world, the consequences of resisting and overcoming temptation spelled out overtly, without the shroud of allegory.

It is possible to perceive a sort of progression in the second half of the poem, a progression steadily away from apparently secularized concerns to increasingly overt Christian symbolism. But the difficulty remains of relating this demonstration of the temptations and struggles of a virtuous life to what has gone before. How does the allegorical Pilgrimage of Life relate to the pragmatic, "real-world" relevance of the debate genre?

No certain answer presents itself. The chief gesture toward unifying these divergent elements is the figure of Dame Sapience, but her role after the debate is largely expository, clarifying for Virtue the significance of what he undergoes. And we recall that in the debate there is an element of equivocation about Sapience, whose apparent significance is not finally rewarded with the victory one might have expected. It is this refusal finally to endorse the values associated with Sapience which may provide some clue as to Hawes's design.

For there is so evident a contrast between the nature of preoccupation in the two parts of the *Example* that it is reasonable to see the differences as deliberate. In the first half, Virtue's role is largely passive as he perceives the enunciation of a series of secular arguments. As he proceeds to action, the poem moves into a different world of moral significance and to a final contemplation of the immutable and eternal. And at the conclusion of this, we turn back immediately from "god the maker of all thynge" (2047) to pray for Him to "saufe kynge Henry our ryghtfull kynge / From all treason" (2049–50). This concluding prayer provides a further link between the two parts. Hawes prays to the "heuenly kynge" for the well-being of the earthly one. Temporal and eternal are joined in a hierarchy of significance that clearly affirms the power of God over man. This is, in effect, the movement of the larger structure of the poem as it proceeds from oblique commentary on political responsibility to a recognition that the path of virtue lies in the commitment to the truth of Christian virtue.

This is what Hawes seems to be attempting to do in the *Example of Virtue,* but the endeavor is only imperfectly reflected in the finished work. The shifts in allegorical technique and its final abandonment suggest an uncertainty of control that creates uncertainties of response. The apparent effort to comment on contemporary events is intermittent. And the structure seems oddly unbalanced.

But the *Example* is not without interest. We see an attempt in it to reflect a moral seriousness that seems to derive from Hawes's sense of his situation within the court as groom of the chamber and hence intimate of Henry VII. The poem appears to be struggling to find an admonitory didactic form that is both poetically appropriate and yet sufficiently tactful. His unease and uncertainty with the allegorical mode as a way of enunciating such concerns is a problem that would recur in other poems, as we will see later in this chapter.

The Conversion of Swearers

Hawes appears to have written the *Conversion of Swearers* sometime between April and June 1509. De Worde's colophon describes Hawes still as groom of the chamber to Henry VII, who died on 21 April of that year. De Worde also designates himself as "prynter vnto ye moost excellent pryncess my lady the kynges graundame" (i.e., Margaret Beaufort), who died in June. It is consequently the last poem Hawes wrote under royal patronage.

The *Conversion* is an extended attack (366 lines in a mixture of rhyme royal and tail rhyme) on those who take Christ's name in vain. Much of the poem is cast in the form of an address by Christ to his audience inviting them to contemplate his sufferings and repent their false swearings. It continues with an enumeration of the consequences to those who fail to pursue a devout life and the blessings to be bestowed upon those who do. The poem concludes with a general reflection of the mutability of earthly affairs, a meditation on Christ's wounds, and a promise of his redemption for those who repent their sins.

This description of the *Conversion* can hardly succeed in reflecting the reasons for its very considerable popularity during the sixteenth century. There are at least four separate editions of it between 1509 and 1551.[10] Thus it shares with the *Pastime of Pleasure* the distinction of being the most frequently reprinted of Hawes's poems.

The reasons for this popularity merit some examination. The subject matter of the poem is an obvious factor. It presents religious sentiments of unexceptionable orthodoxy and piety about an issue which had received extensive treatment in religious art and literature during the Middle Ages. As Rosemary Woolf has shown, there existed before Hawes a developed tradition of complaints against those who swore by parts of Christ's body.[11] The evident demand for editions of Hawes's poem on the subject indicates it was still a topic that could excite interest and concern during the sixteenth century. Indeed, the *Conversion of Swearers* is the only recorded complete poem on this issue.[12]

At least as important as the subject matter was the way in which Hawes chose to explore his concern. The poem contrives to be both dramatic and concrete. Christ appears in his own person, presenting the consequences of his suffering at the hands of those who take his name in vain. He does so in vivid terms:

> Behold my body with blody droppes endewed
> Within your realmes nowe torne so pyteously
> Towsed and tugged with othes cruelly
> Some my heed some myn armes and face
> Some my herte do all to rente and race

> They newe agayne do hange me on the rode
> They tere my sydes and are nothynge dysmayde
> My woundes they open and deuoure my blode
> I god and man moost wofully arayde
> To you complayne it may not be denayde
> ye nowe to tug me ye tere me at the roote
> yet I to you am chefe refuyte and boote.
>
> (80–91)

The dramatic immediacy of such personification is sustained and elaborated by aspects of the poem's style. The *Conversion* employs metrical variation in its middle section. Lines 113–56 depart from Hawes's general rhyme royal and use instead a form of tail rhyme. This tail-rhyme section is accompanied in de Worde's first edition by a woodcut of Christ's sufferings which forms an *imago pietatis*, an "image of piety," to accompany the text. The metrical variation at this point serves to emphasize and reinforce the effect of this visual image. The lines steadily increase in length from one to six syllables and then are equally steadily reduced to one syllable again.

The use of tail rhyme has led to some confusion among later critics. Tail rhyme is "a structure of rhymed lines based on the repetition of a rhyme after the interval of at least two rhyming lines, e.g. *aabaab*."[13] De Worde, in common with other early printers, printed the *b* rhymes for each stanza not directly below the *a* rhymes, as is now invariably done with verse, but *opposite* them. This practice has led to the *Conversion* being viewed as a "pattern poem" of the kind developed most notably in the seventeenth century by George Herbert, where the lines have a shape conforming to their subject matter.[14] Some critics have tried to suggest that Hawes here had a similar intention to "pattern" his verses.[15] But this has clearly been shown to be incorrect.[16] The shape of the poem on the page is a printer's convention, not part of the aesthetic design of the poem.

More interesting is the *poetic* effect of the tail rhyme. It serves to give a measured deliberateness to the actual utterances of Christ, linking the increased extremity of his sufferings to the increased length of lines:

> My face ryght red
> Myn armes spred
> My woundes bled
> (thynke none oder

> Beholde thou my syde
> Wounded so ryght wyde
> Bledynge sore that tyde
> (all for thyn owne sake
> Thus for the I smerted
> Why arte thou harde herted
> Be by me conuerted
> (and thy swerynge aslake . . . .
>
> (125–36)

Suffering is not simply depicted physically but enacted emotionally as Christ's exhortations become more emphatic—and longer in lines—as he perceives man's indifference to what he is enduring because of man. Both imagery and meter sustain and complement homiletic purpose.

And the poem's conclusion adds a new verbal/visual element in the form of an elaborate pun which links the picture of Christ's wounds, man's indifference, and the nature of the Divine sacrifice:

> With my blody woundes I dyde your chartre seale
> Why do you tere it why do ye breke it so
> Syth it to you is the eternall heale
> And the releace of euerlastynge wo
> Behold this lettre with the prynte also
> Of myne owne seale by perfyte portrayture
> Prynte it in mynde and ye shall helthe recure.
>
> (346–52)

The play on "prynte" (350, 352) emphasizes its dual meanings here of "picture" and "imprint" and the interconnection between them: the contemplation of the picture with its "perfyte portrayture" should lead to an imprinting of its meaning in the heart of the beholder. It is linked to the pun on "seale" (346, 351), also both a verb and an object. Christ's blood seals the promise of redemption, an action which for sinful man can be confirmed by the contemplation of the "seal," the picture of his sufferings. The poem shows in such ways an adroit and apposite use of language not generally characteristic of Hawes.

Not all the poem is as successful. Hawes includes his characteristic passage of extended anaphora (234–88) divided equally into admonition ("Wo worthe . . .") and a versification of the Beatitudes ("Blessed be ye . . ."). The transition from dramatic exhortation to straightforward homily is abrupt and jarring, lessening the effect of what is, in many respects, one of Hawes's most successful poems.

There are other aspects to it which are perplexing in light of the underlying conventional piety of the *Conversion*. Chief among these is the question of the poem's audience. The poem contains a number of addresses to rulers and members of the nobility. Christ speaks initially to "ryght myghty princes of euery crysten regyon" (57). A little later he exhorts "ye kynges reygnynge in renowne / Refourme your seruauntes in your courte abused" (92–93). He plays on the difference between his kingship and that of "worldly kynges":

> The wordly kynges hauynge the soueraynte
> ye do well obey without resystence
> ye dare not take theyr names in vanyte
> But with grete honoure and eke reuerence
> Than my name more hye of magnyfycence
> ye ought more to drede whiche am kynge of all
> Bothe god and man and reygne celestyall.
> (192–98)

In the concluding lines Christ again admonishes "ye kynges and lordes of renowne / Exhorte your seruauntes theyr swerynge to cease" (353–54). This reiterated address is too insistent to be ignored. It appears most likely that Hawes's poem is directed, at least primarily, to the circle of Henry VII's court, a circle of which he was still a member. We see him apparently adopting an attitude of explicit disapproval toward certain members of that circle. Such an attitude is quite consistent with Hawes's tendency to overt admonition of those in positions of greater worldly power than he has. It is a tendency that would not necessarily endear him to the new king Henry VIII.

A Joyful Meditation

A Joyful Meditation is the shortest of Hawes's poems (217 lines in 31 rhyme-royal stanzas). It is also the only poem which can be linked to a specific occasion. As its title makes clear it was composed to mark the "coronacyon of our moost natural soucrayne lorde kynge Henry the eyght" which took place on 24 June 1509.

The poem falls into several distinct sections: a prologue in which Hawes invokes the example of Lydgate, who dedicated some of his works to Henry's "worthy predecessour" Henry V; a survey of the reign and achievements of Henry VII; an invocation to the eight planetary deities; a series of prayers to various persons and estates; and a final dedication to the king and an apology by Hawes for his poetic inadequacy.

The poem is an odd one in most respects. Scholarship has been largely content to ignore it and the only comment has been disparaging.[17] There seems no clear structure or overall coherence. There is a general thematic preoccupation with ideas of harmony and continuity, in which the marriage of Henry Tudor and Elizabeth of York is seen as heralding an era of unity. God is praised because

> Two tytles in one thou dydest wel vnyfye
> Whan the rede rose toke the whyte in maryage
> Reygnynge togyder ryght hygh and noblye
> From whose vnyd tytyls and worthy lygnage
> Descended is by ryght excellent courage
> Kynge Henry the .viii. for to reygne doutles
> Vnyversall his fame honour and larges.
>
> (36–42)

This concern with unity provides the basis for the various prayers that follow for continued peace and stability.

Such sentiments may seem an unexceptionable response to a coronation by a poet and courtier, albeit a not very clearly constructed one. But Hawes does not limit himself to such decorous expressions, for running through his poem as a muted counterstatement to his ostensible theme is a recurrent preoccupation with an issue we have encountered already—Henry VII's avarice.

This concern first shows itself early in the poem when Hawes feels it proper to speak of Henry VIII's father, in terms that are hard to see as laudatory:

> Our late souerayne his fader excellent
> I knowe ryght well some holde oppynyon
> That to auaryce he had entendement
> Gadrynge grete rychesse of this his regyon

But they lytell knowe by theyr small reason
For what hye entente he gadered doutles
Vnto his grace suche innumerable ryches

For I thynke well and god had sente hym lyfe
As they haue meruaylled moche of this gadrynge
So it to them shold haue ben affyrmatyfe
To haue had grete wonder of his spendynge
It may fortune he thought to haue mouynge
Of mortall warre our fayth to stablysshe
Agaynst the turkes theyr power to mynysshe.

(71–84)

If the most compelling defense of Henry VII's avarice Hawes can offer is Henry's professed desire to make war against the heathen Turks, then it is hard to know why he would have mentioned it. It is clear that at the time of Henry VIII's coronation the issue of his father's greed was a particularly sensitive one. One of the first acts of the new king was to arrest and subsequently execute in 1510 Henry VII's financial advisors, Sir Richard Empson and Edmund Dudley. Hawes seems to allude to this when he talks of the punishment of those "delytynge them in the synne of auaryce" (95). He alludes to the subject even more explicitly a little later:

On our kynges counsayll downe sende and renue
The trouthe of Iustyce that they may extue
For to do wrong by the synne of couetyce
That here before hathe done grete preiudyce.

(137–40)

And with even greater insistence he returns to the question of Empson and Dudley near the end of the poem:

All ye offycers of euery degree
Beware extorcyon for and it be knowen
No doute it is but ye shall punysshed be
Take hede of them the whiche be ouerthrowen
Remembre well how fortune hathe blowen
The promoters downe and castynge them full lowe
In followynge them ye shall fall as I trowe.

(190–96)

It is clear that Hawes was not alone among the court circle in criticizing the fiscal policies of his late master, which were, as we saw in chapter 2, notably rapacious. Thomas More presented a manuscript collection of epigrams to Henry VIII on the occasion of his coronation, the first one of which is "A Poetical Expression of Good Wishes" to the new king. It includes the following passage on contemporary reaction to the new reign:

Now each man happily does not hesitate to show the possessions which in the past his fear kept hidden in dark seclusion. Now there is enjoyment in any profit which managed to escape the many very sly clutching hands of the many thieves. No longer is it a criminal offence to own property which was honestly acquired (formerly it was a serious offence). No longer does fear whisper, whisper secrets in one's ear. . . .[18]

And there are other contemporary accounts which stress the abuses of the past with equal vigor.[19] Hawes's attacks are not in themselves unusual either in their response to the accession of Henry VIII or in terms of his own frequently expressed concerns about the "synne of auaryce," particularly in the *Pastime of Pleasure* but also in *The Example of Virtue*. What may seem a discordant note in his praise of the new king seems no more than representative of the feelings of the time.

An appreciation of this fact does not serve to mitigate the poem's deficiencies. In fact, a part of its interest lies in the way it manifests some of Hawes's recurrent problems with structure in his poems. Here, as elsewhere, he is unable to impose a form on his material that enables him to integrate anticipatory praise of Henry VIII with retrospective criticism of his father. The two elements remain in jarring discord. It is noteworthy that even when he casts aside the obliquity of allegory for overt statements of criticism Hawes cannot find a form that will encompass what he has to say. The result is a work that is disjointed: the poet's attitudes and feelings are communicated in an intermittent and ambiguous way. His efforts to communicate such feelings at all anticipate his more ambitious endeavors to deal with his own experience and feelings in the *Comfort of Lovers*.

But it is a poem of little distinction. Its interest is largely limited to historical and biographical facts, to the light it sheds on contemporary reactions to events surrounding the coronation of Henry VIII and its reaffirmation of strongly held views that Hawes expresses elsewhere. Thus one must assume that one impulse prompting Hawes to write the poem would be the hope of gaining preferment under Henry VIII. Doubtless he would have expected that appropriate praise might have led to his position as Groom of the Chamber under Henry VII being renewed by his son. If so, he appears to have been disappointed. The reasons for such nonpreferment are unclear and it is impossible to determine whether *A Joyful Meditation* played any part. Indeed, for any information, however scant, about Hawes's career after Henry VIII's accession it is necessary to turn to his final, most obscure poem, *The Comfort of Lovers*.

The *Comfort of Lovers*

The *Comfort of Lovers* is the last of Hawes's surviving poems. We gather from the title of the only recorded edition that it was written "In the seconde yere of the reygne of . . . Henry the eyght," i.e. 1510/11, two years after the publication of his previous poem, *A Joyful Meditation*. The only surviving edition, however, was published ca. 1515. As with the *Example of Virtue* and *The Pastime of Pleasure* there seems to have been some considerable delay between composition and publication.

In certain respects, the *Comfort of Lovers* is consistent with Hawes's other long poems. It is written in his usual rhyme royal (938 lines in 134 stanzas) and poses similar problems in determining the relationship of its structural components. The poem begins with a characteristic prologue in which Hawes seeks to place himself in the tradition of Lydgate. This is followed by an astrological allusion setting the poem in May or June: "Whanne fayre was phebus with his bemes bryght / Amyddes of gemyny" (29–30). At this time we encounter a lover, alone and "musyng in a medowe grene" (36), sorrowing over his suffering and invoking various biblical precedents to strengthen his constancy. He falls asleep and dreams he is in a "goodly gardyn" (64) where he meets a lady to whom he recounts his grief at the loss of his love, and the difficulties he has encountered in continuing to write. This lady directs him to a "goodly toure" (219). He enters this elaborately decorated building and bewails his situation once more.

Suddenly he sees three magic mirrors. From one hangs a sword; from the second a flower in which is set an emerald; from the third "an ymage

. . . of the holy goost" (452–53). Both the second and third mirrors are accompanied by "scrypture" which the dreamer reads. After doing so he sees beside him a sword and shield, which he takes up. Then, after a lament for the loss of his lady, he meets her. A dialogue follows between "Amour" (the dreamer) and "Pucell" (the lady) which concludes with "Pucell" affirming that Venus and Fortune must settle the fate of their love between them. "Amour" agrees and then wakes up, to write the poem describing his dream.

This summary makes clear the now familiar problems with the poem: an arbitrary juxtaposition of situations that lack any clear causality or overall relationship to a discernible pattern of coherent exposition. But in this case the problems of an enigmatic structure are compounded by the insistently cryptic nature of much of the poem's allusion. Such allusiveness is not, of course, peculiar to the *Comfort of Lovers* among Hawes's poems. But its degree and obliquity are so pronounced as to suggest that Hawes is talking on a number of occasions about circumstances that bear directly on his own life and experiences.

The most overt statement of such a connection comes near the end of the poem when Pucell observes to Amour:

> Of late I saw a boke of your makynge
> Called the pastyme of pleasure which is wondrous
> For I thynke and you had not ben in louynge
> Ye coude neuer haue made it so sentencyous
> I redde there all your passage daungerous
> Wherfore I wene for the fayre ladyes sake
> That ye dyd loue ye dyde that boke so make.
>
>   (785–91)

This clearly identifies the protagonist with the author of the *Pastime of Pleasure,* just as the names of the characters here recall the main figures of the earlier poem, Graunde Amour and La Belle Pucelle.

This passage provides an invitation to extend the autobiographical frame of reference to several very obscure passages from the earlier part of the poem. When the dreamer, Amour, initially makes his complaint, he outlines the causes of his sorrow in these terms:

> Thretened with sorowe of many paynes grete
> Thre yeres ago my ryght hande I dyde bynde
> From my browes for fere the dropes doune dyde sweet
> God knoweth all it was nothynge my mynde
> Vnto no persone I durst my herte vntwynde
> yet the trouthe knowynge the good gretest P
> Maye me releace of all my p p p thre.
>
> (134–40)

There is simply no symbolic or allegorical context that gives any meaning to these statements. Before attempting any biographical elucidation it might be helpful to glance at a couple of other passages that seem related to this one, not least in their obscurity of allusion.

A little later the dreamer alludes to another source of grief:

> Aboue .xx. woulues dyde me touse and rent
> Not longe agone delynge moost shamefully
> That by theyr tuggynge my lyfe was nere spent
> I dyde perceyue somwhat of theyr entente
> As the trouthe is knowen vnto god aboue
> My ladyes fader they dyde lytell loue.
>
> (163–68)

Once again, the force of much of the allusion is lost through its inaccessibility. What is the significance of the ".xx. woulues"? Who is "my ladyes fader"? And what is meant by "my lyfe was nere spent"? The poem offers no explicit answers to such questions, nor does it to a passage a little later in the poem, a passage which once again seems to focus self-consciously on Hawes's identity and role as poet. He complains that

> Some had wened for to haue made an ende
> Of my bokes before they hadde begynnynge
> But all vayne they dyde so comprehende
> Whan they of them lacke vnderstandynge
> Vaynfull was & is theyr mysse contryuynge
> Who lyst the trouthe of them for to ensue
> For the reed and whyte they wryte full true.
>
> (183–89)

To which the lady replies:

> . . . I haue perceueraunce
> Of your bokes whiche that ye endyte
> So as ye saye is all the cyrcumstaunce
> Vnto the hyghe pleasure of the reed and whyte
> Which hath your trouth and wyll you acquyte
> Doubte ye no thynge.

(190–95)

These passages do not exhaust the allusive difficulties of the *Comfort of Lovers,* but, taken together, for all their cryptic quality and uncertain syntax they do seem to provide some autobiographical statement that can be tentatively glossed.

It would seem that Hawes had been subjected to some constraints on writing poetry: "Thre yeres ago my ryght hande I dyde bynde" (135). The significance of the time span is not clear. The only poems of Hawes that can be certainly dated between the *Pastime of Pleasure* (1505/6) and the *Comfort of Lovers* (1510/11) are two short poems—the *Conversion of Swearers* and *A Joyful Meditation,* both published in 1509.[20] It may be that Hawes is referring to a period of poetic activity within the court that terminated prior to Henry VII's death in 1509. Hawes is not listed among those members of the court who received mourning on Henry's death, which may imply that he had already left the court circle.

Certainly the other allusions suggest that he had in some way incurred the violent disapproval of someone in a position of power and influence, sufficient to endanger his life ("by theyr tuggynge my lyfe was nere spent") by the attack of ".xx. woulues." This disapproval seems in some way connected with "the good gretest P" (139), presumably an allusion to the Pucell who appears later in the poem.[21] The "p p p thre" (140) seems to refer to some form of suffering, here appropriately alliterative ("pain" . . . "poverty" . . . "passion," for example); it might also allude to each of the three years when he was deprived of his pen when his "right hand" was "bound." It seems also to have led to efforts to suppress some of his writings (cf. 183–89) for reasons that seem to involve "the reed and whyte" (189, 193) a reference to the Houses of York and Lancaster joined by the marriage of Henry Tudor and Elizabeth of York. Once again, the implication seems to be some loss of court favor, against which he protests by affirming his loyalty.

There are additional suggestions that Hawes had been subjected to some loss of status. When Amour encounters Pucell after winning the gifts from the three mirrors, she observes:

> I denye not but that our dedes do shewe
> By meruaylous prowes truly your gentylnesse
> To make you a carter there were not a fewe.
>   (841–43)

She goes on to explain that she is "promest to a myghty lorde" (861), implying that Hawes's humbler social status was a factor disqualifying him from Pucell's love. He may even have been imprisoned. At one point he remarks that "they shall haue sorowe that shytte me in a cage" (565). But to speculate further would be unwarrantable. There is no evidence to substantiate the assertion that the object of Hawes's affections was Mary Tudor, the daughter of Henry VII.[22] That he was in love with someone of a higher status and that there were impediments to his suit, however, seems clear.

It would seem that the poem is concerned to depict, in some way, the experience of Hawes's personal frustration both as poet and lover, possibly compounded by a loss of royal favor. This frustration may have involved some conflict with the other court poets. In some deeply obscure lines near the end of the poem Amour asserts:

> Surely I thynke I suffred well the phyppe
> The nette also dydde teche me on the waye
> But me to bere I trowe they lost a lyppe
> For the lyfte hande extendyd my Iournaye
> And not to call me for my sporte and playe
> Wherfore by foly yf that they do synne
> The holy goost maye well the batayle wynne.
>   (890–96)

The notion of "the lyfte hande" (893) seems designed to recall the earlier mention of his "right hand" (135) and to be linked to the earlier intimations of Hawes's involuntary silence. The recent editors of the *Comfort of Lovers* may be right in suggesting some connection between these lines and Hawes's fellow poet John Skelton, especially in the mention of "the phyppe," a contracted form of Philip, a name for a sparrow. This may be a reference to Skelton's poem *Philip Sparrow* and by extension to its author in terms that could imply some conflict.[23] The phrase "they lost a lyppe" would seem to suggest that Hawes was the loser in this conflict and was forced into silence. But this must remain the merest conjecture, given the inaccessibility of the allusion.

The texture of personal allusion in the poem also finds other forms of expression, particularly through different forms of play upon Hawes's identity as the author of the *Pastime of Pleasure*. As we have seen, Pucell explicitly links Amour/Hawes to this poem. But there are a number of covert references of different kinds. There are a number of lines which either copy or echo lines from the *Pastime* in the *Comfort of Lovers*.[24] One would not, in isolation, wish to make much of this, given Hawes's tendency to self-borrowing. As we have seen, the *Pastime* itself borrows often from the earlier *Example of Virtue*. But the possibility here of some self-conscious allusiveness is strengthened by a number of apparent punning references to the title of the *Pastime,* playing particularly with the idea of "past time."

Such apparent puns recur through the *Comfort of Lovers*—for example, "Dyspeyre you not for no thynge that is past" (83); "Passe ye tyme here accordynge to your lykynge / It maye fortune your lady of excellence / wyll passe her tyme here" (247–49); ". . . Remembrynge well my dedes done in tymes past" (345); "Alas he sayth what nedeth to deuyse / Ony suche pastyme here for to repayre" (626–27); "I am as past your loue to specify" (818); "Ye knowe what I am ye knowe my loue is past" (833); "Nothynge is past but that fortunes pleasure / May call it agayne in the tyme future" (839–40); "My loue is past it can not be forsaken" (899); "The snares and nettes set in sondrye maner / Doone in tyme past made many a bryde a dawe" (904–5); "From daye to daye theyr pastyme to attende" (937). The title of the *Pastime of Pleasure* becomes a reference point for the poetic and the personal dimensions of Hawes's identity; it provides a recurrent reminder to his audience of his central poetic achievement while simultaneously recalling the adverse effects of the changes of time on his personal circumstances.

The structure of the poem also insists on this consciousness of the significance of time past. At the beginning of the *Comfort of Lovers* Amour's thoughts are firmly rooted in the past, in the memory of his love: "Dyuers yeres ago I dyde in mynde retayne / A lady yonge a lady fayre of syght" (89–90), he complains. His meeting with the "lady of goodly age" (76) leads to the detailed rehearsal of his past sufferings and losses. It is she, however, who introduces the first prospect of futurity and hence of hope into the poem. Indeed, this is a refrain of all her utterances. She asserts that: "Doubt ye no thynge but god wyll so agre / That at the last ye shal your lady see" (153–54); or again, "Doubte ye no thynge but at the last ye maye / Of your true mynde yet fynde a Ioyfull daye" (195–96); and "No doubte it is that god so hyghe and stronge / Ful meruaylously wyl soone reuenge theyr wronge" (216–17). The clear parallelism of these pronouncements emphasizes once again the poem's concerns with time, setting the promise of future vindication against Amour's past sufferings.

These several aspects of time—past, present, and future—are systematically elaborated in the symbolism of the three mirrors Amour sees in the "goodly toure" (219) to which he is conducted. The first of these mirrors reflects his past. He sees "how I had ledde my lyfe / Sythens the tyme of my dyscrecyon" (323–24), "remembrynge well my dedes done in tymes past" (345). This is the only one of the mirrors at which Amour does not receive a gift. Instead, he is invited to contemplate the hanging sword "poynt dounwarde ryght harde and asperous" (319), symbolizing the consequences of Amour's life previously "folowynge the pleasure of wylfull amonycyon / Not vnto vertue hauynge intencyon" (326–27). The hanging sword will be the fate of those who do not repent for past errors before it is too late (340–42).

Amour's experiences before the other mirrors are rather different. The second mirror signifies self-knowledge: "In this myrour . . . / Thou shalt well lerne thy selfe for to knowe" (365–66). He comes to an understanding of his past and the need to trust in God's purposes:

> I sawe there trappes I sawe theyr gynnes all
> I thanked god than the swete holy goost
> whiche brought me hyder so well in specyall
> withoute whiche myrour I had ben but loost

In god aboue the lorde of myghtes moost
I put my trust.

                                        (407–12)

This achievement of present self-knowledge and the correct orientation of Amour's priorities are represented by the gift that accompanies the mirror, the "floure of golde ryght fyne" (351), which "who so dooth it bere / . . . his syght shal not mynyshe" (379–80).

The third mirror seems to symbolize the promise of the future. It is surmounted by "an ymage . . . / Of the holy goost" (452–53). And in it Amour sees "the fyrmament" (536) and a "meruaylous sterre" (538) which "sygnyfyeth the resynge of a knyght" (547) and the defeat of his enemies. This defeat is to be effected through the gifts accompanying the mirror, the sword of "prepudence" (512) and the shield of "perceueraunce" (520). It is not possible to be certain of the precise significance of either of these terms, especially the first, which is not discussed or glossed by the poem's editors. But they seem to mean, respectively, "foresight"[25] and both "understanding" and "endurance."[26] Presumably these are the qualities required to carry Amour to triumph over his enemies.

It is easy to see that the episode of the three mirrors extends and makes explicit an underlying preoccupation with time. The episode itself is a pivotal one. It lies between Amour's sorrowful past, as recounted to the lady, and the possibility of a future which is reflected in his next encounter, his dialogue with Pucell herself.

The dialogue between the two lovers is totally curious. It is perhaps ironic that, in one sixteenth-century manuscript, extracts from this section should have been reworked to form a separate love poem.[27] For the mood of the dialogue in the *Comfort of Lovers* itself is one that lacks any intensity of emotion. Such emotion as there is seems hardly celebratory, but controlled once again by the perspective of time, being either retrospectively reflective or hopefully anticipatory.

At the outset Amour's attitude is retrospective: "Ryght longe ago your beaute sodanly / Entred my mynde and hath not syth dekayed" (810–11). And as we have already seen, this section of the poem contains numerous references to "time past." But Pucell seems to remain fixed on the future—"They have me promest to a myghty lorde" (861). Her attitude to Amour seems to be one of helpless affection—"For ye knowe well what case that I am yn / Peryllous it wolde be or that ye coude me wyne" (776–77) she says; and she insists his love for her is hopeless: "I am as past your loue to specyfy / Why wyll ye loue where is no remedy" (818–19).

But in its later stages the attitudes and tone of the dialogue change. The moment of this change can be pinpointed quite precisely. It takes place when Amour speaks these words: "Madame in the worlde ben but thynges twayne / As loue and hate ye knowe your selfe the trouthe" (862–63). These lines are clearly intended to recall ones near the beginning of the *Comfort of Lovers*. In conversation with the "lady of goodly age" Amour observes: "In all this worlde ben but thynges twayne / As loue and hate the trouth for to tell" (120–21).

While these allusions seem intended to recall one another, there are important contextual differences. In the earlier one Amour goes on:

> And yf I sholde hate my lady certayne
> Than worthy I were to dye of deth cruell
> Seynge all ladyes that she doth excell
> In beaute grace prudence and mekenes.
> (122–25)

Here we have an unambiguous affirmation of enduring love. But by the time he reiterates it, the aphorism has acquired a rather different force. This time, after uttering it, he continues:

> yf I sholde hate you deth I were worthy playne
> Than had you cause with me to be wrothe
> To deserue dysplesure my herte wolde be lothe
> wherfore fayre lady I yelde at this hower
> To your mekenes my herte my loue and power.
> (864–68)

The affirmation of constancy in love remains. But the onus of responsibility is now shifted to Pucell herself. Amour "yelde[s]" to her "mekenes." His attitude is now calmer, more reflective. He professes himself "content to tary" (880), seeming to accept Pucell's advice, "be ye pacyent" (887).

In the end, they both agree to follow the course outlined by Pucell:

> I do now submytte
> My wyll and thought to the lady Venus
> As she is goddesse and doth true loue knytte
> Ryght so to determyne the mater betwene vs
> With assent of fortune so good and gracyous
> Besechynge you now for to holde you styll
> For these two ladyes maye your mynde fulfyll.
>   (911–17)

Amour seems to have shifted to a posture of disciplined reasonableness; as he observes, "Examples past dooth teche one to withdrawe / Frome all suche perylles wherefore than maye I / . . . beware full parfytly" (908–10). It may seem strange that Amour should submit this aspect of destiny to Venus and Fortune, deities of equivocal reputation generally identified with the mutability of human affairs. But it seems that by such a submission Amour is recognizing the loss of his love. His final words are "forget me not . . . remember me" (922, 924).

At this point, Amour awakes. The poem ends immediately with an envoy directing his "lytell treatyse" to "euery lady" and

> Besechynge them to remember truely
> How thou doost purpose to do thy dylygence
> To make suche bokes by true experyence
> From daye to daye theyr pastyme to attende
> Rather to dye thou than wolde them offende.
>   (934–38)

It is hard to avoid the suspicion of irony here. Amour "make[s] suche bokes by true experyence" to be a "pastyme" or entertainment for such ladies. When he exhorts them to "remember truely" (which can mean "faithfully" or "constantly"), it is easy to recall that the poem explores "true experience" of the author of the *Pastime,* experience which has been the very opposite of a "pastime" because of such a lady as the poem now addresses.

For all its allusive difficulties it is possible to discern an apparent design to the *Comfort of Lovers.* Several interrelated strands of concern run through it: frustration in love, frustration in personal achievement, and the effects of time on attitude and understanding appear to be the major issues it seeks to explore. We follow the protagonist as he achieves a new philosophic stance that turns his attention from contemplation of earlier loss and suffering through, in effect, making these the topic of his poem. The conclusion does not offer a happy ending, or even the possibility of one. But what the poem does do is provide a justification of the poet/lover, by rehearsing the injustices to which he has been subjected, affirming his worth (in the three mirrors episode), and presenting him as a faithful, albeit frustrated, lover.

But the poem remains for us a frustrating if not a perplexing one. It does seem to mark a new stage in Hawes's work in which personal complaint becomes more overt and central to the design of the poem than was the case in earlier poems. As the recent editors of it have observed, the *Comfort of Lovers* seems to be "an attempt at intimacy, at personal revelation, at coping with large problems both personal and political,"[28] employing the resources of a medieval poetic to new and not wholly successful ends. The trappings of the dream vision, the abrupt intrusions of obscure allegory, and the characteristically elusive/allusive character of Hawes's diction combine to cast a fair degree of obscurity over many aspects of the poem.

Against these not uncharacteristic failures may be set Hawes's innovative reworking of the medieval genre of complaint poems. He gives to a form of generalized lament a new particularization, a personal frame of reference that makes it, in effect, a new form in English verse—the autobiographical poem. Hawes's experiment in the form is fumbling and uncertain. The perspectives he offers us on what he has to say seem generally either too close to be fully comprehensible or too distanced to have any clear applicability at all. At one extreme we have the largely inaccessible personal reflections, at the other the stylizations of allegory. Such characteristic structural uncertainties limit Hawes's achievement in the *Comfort of Lovers,* but do not negate it. It remains an intriguing attempt to explore new poetic territory, new not simply for Hawes but for English poetry.

What reaction, if any, there was to Hawes's complaint is not known. After the *Comfort of Lovers* he is lost from view forever. It is tantalizing that he should have done so at the very moment when he was beginning to sound an individual voice that attempted to make personal experience the subject matter of poetry.

Chapter Four

Reputation, Influence, and Achievement

Posthumous Reputation and Influence

We do not know when Hawes died. It seems reasonable to assume that he was dead by the early 1520s at the latest. His posthumous reputation and influence do only a little to offset the obscurity that surrounds his actual life.

An important figure in Hawes's posthumous reputation, as during his life, was Wynkyn de Worde, his publisher. While Hawes was probably still alive he reprinted the *Conversion of Swearers* (ca. 1510) and the *Pastime of Pleasure* (1517), correcting the garbled passages of the Godfrey Gobelive episode that appeared in the 1509 edition.[1] De Worde also twice reprinted the *Example of Virtue* in (?) 1520 and 1530. The (?) 1520 edition only survives in a fragment, but the 1530 edition is very curious and sheds some light on de Worde's concern with Hawes's reputation.

There are over three hundred changes to the 1530 text from the 1509 one. These changes are not easy to account for, since in many cases they involve extensive rewriting of parts of Hawes's text.[2] But careful examination suggests that they are likely to be the work of de Worde himself. The changes tend to lessen the obscurities of Hawes's language, syntax, and style, altering these aspects when they were apparently adjudged too archaic for a contemporary audience.

Such concerns with clarity and contemporaneity are evident in de Worde's treatment of earlier texts.[3] What is curious is that he should have subjected the work of a recent poet to such modernization. Clearly he felt the effort worthwhile to try to keep Hawes's poem accessible to his audience.

De Worde also seems to have prompted others within his circle to posthumous praise of Hawes. The only two direct references to Hawes in the years after his death come from versifiers who have a clear connection with Hawes's publisher. The first of these is by Thomas Feylde, in his poem *A Contrauersye bytwene a louer and a Iaye* (ca. 1529), which was printed by de Worde. In the prologue he mentions

> Young STEPHEN HAWES whose soul GOD pardon!
> Treated of Love so clerkly and well
> To read his Works is mine affection,
> Which he compiled for *La belle Pucelle.*
> Remembering stories fruitful and delectable;[4]

Feylde's regard for Hawes's *Pastime* ("*La belle Pucelle*") is evident. Hawes is joined with earlier "laureate Poets" mentioned in the prologue such as Chaucer ("Flower of rhetoric eloquence") and the "famous Rhetorician" Lydgate.

He is similarly linked to these major medieval poets in Robert Copland's prologue to de Worde's edition of Chaucer's *The assemble of fowles,* published in 1530. The prologue contains the following passage:

> Chaucer is deed the whiche this pamphlete wrate
> So ben his heyres in all suche besynesse
> And gone is also the famous clerke Lydgate
> And so is yonge Hawes god theyr soules adresse.[5]

The chief interest of the passage is its further indication of Hawes's reputation with de Worde's circle. Copland was a close associate of de Worde's for many years, and could conceivably have known Hawes himself. And the appearance of two such eulogies in (probably) consecutive years provides some indication of the solicitude of this circle for his reputation, evident in the unselfconscious linking of his name with those of Chaucer and Lydgate.[6]

It is possible that de Worde had some cause to rue his enthusiastic sponsorship. An inventory of his stock in 1553, nearly twenty years after his death, includes fifty copies of the *Conversion of Swearers.*[7] Since de Worde had published his second edition of this poem about 1510, it might be felt that his own appreciation of Hawes's poetry was not necessarily shared by many of his contemporaries.

Yet it was the only one of Hawes's works that other contemporary printers felt worth publishing. The *Conversion of Swearers* was reprinted by John Butler about 1530 and Robert Toye in 1551. None of Hawes's other works appears to have been reprinted until the mid-1550s when the *Pastime of Pleasure* was reprinted twice, by Wayland in 1554 and Tottel in 1555. The former edition contains a beguiling preface which includes the following passage:

I offer here vnto the for thy better instruction this little volume conteynynge and treatyng vpon the seuen liberall sciences & the whole course of mans lyfe, first compiled & deuised by Stephen Hawes . . . A man (as by his worckes appeareth) of a pleasaunte wytte, and singuler learnynge, wherin thou shalt finde at one tyme, wisdome and learnynge, with myrthe and solace. So that thou mayest easelye fynde (as it were in pastyme) wythout offence of nature that thyng, and in short space, whiche many great clarkes wythout great paynes and trauayle, & long continuance of time heretofore could neuer obteyne nor get.[8]

Wayland's notion that the *Pastime* combined pleasure and profit in a "little volume" does not seem to have gained much ground. After Tottel's 1555 edition neither the *Pastime of Pleasure* nor any of Hawes's other works would be reprinted until the nineteenth century.

Hawes's works do not seem to have created any extensive manuscript tradition, either before or after publication. The *Pastime of Pleasure* may have circulated in some form in manuscript, but if so, it now seems lost.[9] It does appear in selected form in two manuscripts. Hunterian MS 230 in Glasgow University Library contains a single stanza.[10] Bodleian Library MS Rawlinson C. 813, a large anthology of late medieval verse, includes several poems which are adaptations of parts of the *Pastime,* generally converting them into love songs and complaints.[11] One such adaptation is particularly interesting in that it adapts and combines parts of the *Pastime* with lines from Hawes's *Comfort of Lovers.* The adaptation seems to have been undertaken for some special occasion, since even specific dates in Hawes's poem are changed.[12] One other poem in this manuscript adapts stanzas from the *Comfort of Lovers* to create a "lover's plaint."[13] It may seem ironic that Hawes's moral and didactic verses should be made to serve the cause of secular love song. He would probably have more readily approved of the only other manuscript appearance of one of his works, the lengthy sequence of anaphora from the *Conversion of Swearers* that appears in British Library MS Harley 4294.[14]

It seems doubtful whether Hawes's works were much read in manuscript. The conclusion of the editors of the *Minor Poems* that "the presence of stanzas from three separate poems in two [i.e., three] distinct manuscripts . . . indicates that Hawes's work was read, re-copied . . . and remembered well into the sixteenth century"[15] is to place an unduly optimistic interpretation on the evidence. Only the Rawlinson manuscript reveals any extended interest in Hawes's poetry. In the other two we simply find brief extracts copied onto manuscript flyleaves. All the indications are that, by the mid-sixteenth century at the latest, Hawes's poetry seems to have lost its audience. And even before that its appeal seems to have been limited.

Signs of specific literary indebtedness to his poetry are similarly meager. As we have seen, Thomas Feylde had read the *Pastime*. In his poem *A Contrauersye betwene a louer and a Iaye* he begins a list of examples of the transitoriness of love with "Grand Amour."[16] An earlier writer who seems to have been influenced by Hawes is William Nevill, whose *Castle of Pleasure* survives only in an edition of 1518 by Pepwell, but which may have been originally published earlier by de Worde. Nevill has been characterized as "branded with the iron of Hawes's formulae and Hawes's vocabulary."[17] Certain details in his poem suggest a specific knowledge of the *Example of Virtue*,[18] but the influence is not striking.

In only one area does Hawes seem to have left any noteworthy impact. His influence has been identified on a number of occasions in the dramatic literature of Tudor England, particularly in the interlude and courtly entertainment. For example, a celebratory tableau for the New Year, presented at Henry VIII's court in 1511, has been suggested to possess some parallels with the *Pastime of Pleasure*.[19] The anonymous *Interlude of Youth,* written about 1513–14, has as one of its major sources the *Example of Virtue.* A number of lines are either borrowed from or echo Hawes's poem, and at least one of the characters, Lady Lechery, may be modeled on the figure of Dame Cleanness in the *Example*.[20]

The most curious evidence of such dramatic interest does not occur until the early 1560s, and was probably occasioned by the reprinting of the *Pastime of Pleasure* in 1554 and 1555. Gerard Leigh's book of arms, the *Accedens of Armoury,* was first published in 1562. It contains[21] a description of parts of the 1561 Christmas revels in the Inner Temple, probably composed by Arthur Broke. As has been noted,[22] the source for these revels is the plot of the *Pastime of Pleasure*: a young man meets Governance and Grace, who direct him to the Tower of Doctrine, where he falls in love with Dame Beauty. Before he can win her he has to seek wisdom. He proceeds to the Tower of Chivalry, and, after being dubbed knight, slays a nine-headed monster, whereupon he marries Dame Beauty. Then, in old age, there appear to him the pageants of Fame, Memory, Time, and Eternity.

It does not, however, seem to have been noticed that the revels reflect a considerably greater acquaintance with the *Pastime* than a knowledge of its plot. The account begins with a punning reference to the title of Hawes's poem: "he ledd me towards the Pallace of his Prince, to passe ye time w^t pleasure"[23] And throughout Leigh draws directly upon phrases and specific details from Hawes. Two examples from Leigh's descriptions of Time and Eternity and the corresponding passages in the *Pastime* demonstrate this (for convenience I have italicized the correspondences in both verse and prose). Time is described thus in Leigh's account:

Thus appeared Forworne Tyme, in darke shape with fashion . . . An olde man, tall, and strong of persone, *hauyng long winges and couered ouer all with Swallowe fethers. In hys ryght hande, a brennynge fyre. In hys left hande, an Horologe, a sworde surely gyrte. Hys legges were in bryghte armour,* and he was marked with the seuen Plannettes in thys wyse. On the hynder part of hys head, was Saturne, *on hys forehead, Iupiter. In hys mouthe Mars, on hys right wynge Sol. On hys left wynge, Mercury. At hys brest was Venus, and aboue hys wast, was horned Diana in ye wane.*[24]

In the *Pastime,* the corresponding passage reads:

> Aged he was with a berd doubtles
> *Of swalowes feders his wynges were longe*
> His body fedred he was hye and strong
>
> *In his lefte hande he had an horology*
> *And in his ryght hande a fyre brennynge*

> A *swerde aboute hym gyrte full surely*
> *His legges armed clerely shynynge*
> And on his noddle derkely flamynge
> Was sette Saturne pale as ony leed
> *And Iupyter a myddes his forhed*
>
> *In the mouthe Mars and in his ryght wynge*
> *Was splendent Phebus* with his golden beames
> *And in his brest there was* resplendysshynge
> The shynynge *Venus* with depured streames
> That all about dyde cast her fyry leames
> *In his left wynge Mercury and aboue his wast*
> *Was horned Dyane her opposycyon past.*
>
> (5611–27)

A little later in Leigh's work Eternity is described:

And whilest he stoode in thys bosting, came *Eternitie, apparailed in whyte vesture, with a triple Emperiall Diademe,* and sayde to him. *First y*ᵉ *hygh God made heauen hys owne dwelling place (although his power is euery where)* and there is Eternitie, where Time may not abide *but is caried alwaies towards his own end. And as my maker had no beginning, so shall I neuer haue ending.*[25]

Once again, this is clearly derived from Hawes's corresponding passage:

> And thus as tyme made his conclusyon
> *Eternyte in a fayre whyte vesture*
> To the temple came with hole affeccyon
> And on her hede a *dyademe ryght pure*
> *With thre crownes* of precyous treasure. . . .
>
> *Fyrst god made heuen his propre habytacle*
> Though that his power be in euery place
> *In eterne heuen is his tabernacle*
> Tyme is there in no maner of cace
> *Tyme renneth alwaye his ende* to enbrace
> *Now I my selfe shall haue none endynge*
> *And my maker had no begynnynge.*
>
> (5747–51, 5754–60)

In both passages we find lines and phrases appropriated verbatim with only minor adjustments in order and the omission or paraphrase of difficult words. This is typical of the method of appropriation employed in this account. It is interesting that several of Hawes's near contemporaries should have been quick to perceive the potential of his works for forms of dramatic adaptation.

The 1550s and early 1560s marked the high watermark of interest in Hawes. In addition to this careful imitation and the reprinting of the *Conversion of Swearers* and the *Pastime* there appeared Bale's biography and bibliography in his *Scriptorum Illustrium Maioris Brytanniae* (1557). But from the early 1560s interest appears to have waned. Holinshed, for example, includes Hawes in his *Chronicles of England* (1578) but seems to lack any specific knowledge of his works, describing him simply as a "learned gentleman, and of such reputation, as he was admitted to be one of the priuie chamber to king Henrie the seuenth."[26]

It is appropriate here to consider the question of the possible relationship between Hawes's poems the *Example of Virtue* and, more particularly, the *Pastime of Pleasure* and Spenser's *Faerie Queene*.[27] There has been a persistent attempt by scholars, from at least the early years of the nineteenth century, to see the *Pastime* as a model for Spenser's poem. The most recent has been C. S. Lewis, who asserted that it is "the English poem which probably influenced him most."[28]

There are some broad correspondences between the two works which could imply Hawes's influence. He seems to have been the first English poet to attempt to combine allegory and romance, a combination to which Spenser was to give such significant form in the later sixteenth century. Such a parallel is striking, but it seems almost certainly coincidental. Efforts to assemble any more detailed correspondences between the two poets have proved unconvincing,[29] and it remains unlikely that Spenser would have been able to read either of Hawes's major allegories even if he had wished to. The *Example of Virtue* was last reprinted in the sixteenth century in 1530; the *Pastime of Pleasure,* in 1555. Spenser was not born until around 1552. It seems doubtful whether copies of either work would have been circulating sufficiently for him to have become aware of them. Hawes's poems may provide suggestive analogues and anticipations of the *Faerie Queene* but direct influence is not likely.

The seventeenth century saw a decline in interest in medieval literature in general and Hawes in particular. The most interesting reference to him appears in Anthony à Wood's *Athenae Oxonienses* (1691–92). This is a biographical account derived almost wholly from Bale, but including on unknown authority the assertion of Hawes's extensive knowledge of Lydgate's poetry (see above, p. 12). Wood concludes that "this author was in great value among ingenious men, in the latter end of Hen. 7"[30] It is indicative of the general neglect that the only edition of the *Pastime* of which Wood was aware was the last (1555) one.

Hawes's stock rose a little during the eighteenth century. This was due largely to a renewed interest in medieval literature among various scholars and antiquarians. George Mason, for example, the first editor of Thomas Hoccleve, possessed copies of the 1517 edition of the *Pastime* and the 1530 edition of the *Example of Virtue*.[31] The unique copies of the 1509 *Pastime* and 1515 *Comfort of Lovers* appear to owe their preservation to Joseph Brereton, sometime fellow of Queen's College, Cambridge, and apparently chaplain to the family of the earl of Dysart.[32] He left a number of annotations in them, some apparently based on Wood's biography. And the poet Thomas Gray was sufficiently interested in Hawes to acquire and annotate a copy of the 1555 edition of the *Pastime*.[33]

One figure stands out, however, in the history of Hawes's reputation in the eighteenth century. It is to Thomas Warton that we owe the first attempts at a critical assessment of Hawes. He seems to have discovered Hawes in the early stages of his researches into early English poetry; there are a number of references in his preliminary manuscript notes.[34] But his first published comments appear in his *Observations on the Fairy Queen of Spenser* (1754), where Hawes is praised as

the restorer of invention. . . . He not only revived but improved the antient allegoric vein . . . Instead of that dryness of description, so remarkably disgusting in many of his predecessors, we are by this poet often entertained with the luxuriant effusions of Spenser. . . . To sum up all, [he] was the first of our poets who decorated invention with perspicuous and harmonious numbers.[35]

Warton's next discussion of Hawes is far more extensive and even more laudatory. It occurs in the second volume of his monumental *History of English Poetry* (1778).[36] He opens his account with the uncompromising assertion that "the only writer deserving of the name of a poet in the reign of Henry the seventh, is Stephen Hawes."[37] The force of this claim is somewhat lessened by the lengthy discussion of the *Temple of Glass* that follows. Warton believes it to be by Hawes (on Bale's authority) when it is actually by Lydgate. But his admiration is even greater for the *Pastime of Pleasure,* which he terms a "capital performance" and "almost the only effort of imagination and invention which had yet appeared in our poetry since Chaucer."[38] After a detailed account of the plot of the poem he concludes that

we must acknowledge, that Hawes has shewn no inconsiderable share of imagination, if not in inventing romantic action, at least in applying and enriching the general incidents of the Gothic fable.[39]

Warton's interest differs from that expressed in his earlier observations. Here he has little to say about style and technique, quoting and commenting on only a couple of stanzas. He seems primarily interested in the plot, the elaboration of the "Gothic fable." More striking than what he says is his evident enthusiasm for Hawes and the length at which he expresses it. In this volume of the *History* only Lydgate receives more space and only Skelton as much among the individual writers discussed, and neither of these receives the unambiguous acclaim Hawes does. Warton's study is a pioneering one, the beginning of critical and scholarly awareness of Hawes's existence. As in so much else in his work his response to Hawes testifies to Warton's independent and highly idiosyncratic enthusiasm for medieval poetry.

Thomas Percy's advocacy of Hawes was more muted, but as befits one of the greatest literary antiquarians of the eighteenth century he clearly had some interest in the poet. He corresponded with Warton on several occasions about Hawes, observing on one occasion that "Hawes's poems would . . . very properly be re-printed."[40] It was apparently through Warton that Percy was able to include an extract from the *Pastime of Pleasure* in the first edition of his *Reliques of Ancient English Poetry* (1765).[41] Apart from the stanzas in Warton's *History* this is the only occasion when any of Hawes's poetry was published during the eighteenth century.

The virtual inaccessibility of Hawes's oeuvre at this time occasioned some comment and complaint. In 1800, Henry Hodgson, another antiquary, addressed a particularly poignant lament on this subject to Percy:

For many years, with the most indefatigable industry, I have endeavoured to obtain, if not the possession, at least the sight, of what I cannot but regard as one of the finest poems in our own or any other language. . . . The poem I mean is Stephen Hawes's "Pastime of Pleasure," which judging from Warton's analysis of it. . . . I cannot but regard as highly superior to any thing that any of our poets, Spenser only excepted, could have produced in the same walk. . . . I cannot help lamenting that . . . Hawes's . . . valuable productions have not met with an editor whose taste, learning, and character in the world might secure them that attention which they merit.[42]

It was to be some time before the situation changed. The early part of the nineteenth century saw this sense of the rarity of Hawes's works confirmed in sale prices. Copies of the early editions seem to have been scarce and expensive. Thomas Dibdin, the great bibliographer and bibliophile, paid the very considerable sum of £81 for a copy of the 1517 edition of the *Pastime* at the sale of the Duke of Roxburghe's library in 1812. At the same sale a copy of the 1530 *Example of Virtue* fetched £61.[43] Even the relatively common 1554 edition of the *Pastime* fetched £40-19-0 at a sale in 1820.[44] In addition to his role as a collector of Hawes, Dibdin has an important place in the history of his scholarship, for in his *Library Companion* (1824) he announced the discovery of the unique, imperfect copy of the 1509 edition of the *Pastime* together with the unique copy of the *Comfort of Lovers,* which, it will be recalled, Joseph Brereton studied in the eighteenth century in Ham House, the residence of the earl of Dysart.[45]

There were also signs of an awakening of literary interest in Hawes in the early part of the nineteenth century. It cannot be said that the earliest comments on him were very encouraging. Thus the antiquary George Ellis took issue with Warton's favorable comments in his *Specimens of the Early English Poets* (London, 1801): "It is . . . very doubtful whether every reader will concur in this favourable opinion of Stephen Hawes's merits," he suggests, going on to put his finger on one of the basic problems of the plot of the *Pastime*: "an accurate knowledge of the seven sciences . . . does not seem to be indispensably requisite to the success of a love adventure." His conclusion is unambiguous:

Throughout the [*Pastime*] Hawes has studiously imitated the style of Lydgate, but he has generally copied his worst manner. He is diffuse, fond of expletives, and his epithets add nothing to the sense.[46]

These are harsh words, and not, in the context, particularly fair ones
Ellis only quotes from a single stanza to illustrate his criticism o
Hawes's style.

But Ellis's criticisms were to gain authoritative endorsement. Si
Walter Scott, reviewing his edition for the *Edinburgh Review* in 1804
dismissed Hawes summarily as "a bad imitator of Lydgate, ten time
more tedious than his original."[47] The poet Thomas Campbell declined
to include Hawes in his *Specimens of the British Poets* (London, 1819), bu
does offer some observations on him in his introduction. He attacks the
"capriciousness and vague moral meaning" and the "puerility" o
Hawes's allegorical romance, as well as the "foolish personage" o
Godfrey Gobelive. He also complains of Graunde Amour's "tiresome"
sojourn at the Tower of Doctrine. "Yet," he goes on, "as the story seems
to be of Hawes' invention, it ranks him above the mere chroniclers and
translators of the age." And he can find "one fine line" to praise in the
Pastime: "The fire was great: it made the island light" (4942).[48]

Fortunately, Hawes was soon to acquire other, less grudging advo-
cates. One of the most notable of these was the poet and scholar Robert
Southey. His *Select Works of the British Poets* (1831) includes virtually all
of the *Pastime of Pleasure,* thus making it available to a wide audience for
the fist time since 1555. His introductory comments, although brief,
leave no doubt as to his view of the poem: "The Pastime of Pleasure . . .
is the best English poem of its century," he announces.[49]

Even more enthusiastic in her advocacy was the poet Elizabeth
Barrett Browning. In 1842, in an article in the *Athenaeum,* she terms
the *Pastime of Pleasure* one of "the four columnar marbles, the four
allegorical poems, on whose foundation is exalted into light the great
allegorical poem of the world, Spenser's 'Faery Queen.'" (The others are
Piers Plowman, Chaucer's *House of Fame,* and Lydgates *Temple of Glass.*)
She goes on to quote admiringly several stanzas, observing that:

He is, in fact, not merely ingenious and fanciful, but abounds—the word,
with an allowance for the unhappiness of his subject, is not too strong—with
passages of thoughtful sweetness and cheerful tenderness, at which we are
constrained to smile and sigh, and both for "pastyme."[50]

Such approval contrasts sharply with the attitude of the tireless
antiquary Thomas Wright, who in 1845 produced the first separate

edition of the *Pastime* since Tottel's. He seems to have approached his task with some distaste:

The *Pastime of Pleasure* . . . is one of those allegorical writings which were popular with our forefathers, but which can now only be looked upon as monuments of the bad taste of a bad age. It is, however, a monument; and being one of the most remarkable productions between the age of Lydgate and that of Wyatt and Surrey, it deserves to be reprinted as one of the links in the history of English literature.[51]

This chill draft of historical relativism does not seem to have gained much support during the latter part of the nineteenth century and early years of the twentieth. There were some further attempts at editions of Hawes's works. David Laing edited *The Conversion of Swearers* and *A Joyful Meditation* for the Abbotsford Club in 1865.[52] And in 1901 Arber produced an edition of the *Example of Virtue,* the first since 1530.[53]

It is also possible to trace a strand of sympathetic response to Hawes running through the critical comments on him during this period. Stopford Brooke, writing in 1880, observed that

Amid many poems, more imitative of Lydgate than of Chaucer, his long allegorical poem, entitled the *Pastime of Pleasure* is the best. In fact, it is the first, since the middle of the fifteenth century, in which Imagination again began to plume her wings and soar.[54]

Henry Morley seems somewhat inclined to share this view, although with a crucial qualification:

Other parts of a true poet, in the care spent on essentials of life, in choice and treatment of his fable, Stephen Hawes had; but if he wrote his lines as they are printed he was not skilled in the mechanism of his art. He was held by the ears when he was dipped in Helicon.[55]

This sense of Hawes as a potential poet, stifled by his metrical ineptitude, is echoed in the criticism of George Saintsbury, especially in his monumental *History of English Prosody* (1908):

Here is Hawes, who actually would be a poet if he could ever get the great ox off his tongue, and who cannot get it to budge more than an inch or so for his life.[56]

After careful analysis of some of Hawes's verses he concludes that

the *Pastime of Pleasure* is in the most dishevelled, out-at-heel and generally slatternly condition, as regards metre and almost all the other consituents of prosody in the widest sense.[57]

But nonetheless he retains some regard for Hawes's poetic achievement, describing him in a later study as "a swan singer of mediaeval music, half graceful, half awkward, as swans are on earth and in water respectively."[58]

The most incisive and approbatory observations on Hawes in this period come from the pen of the notoriously hard-to-please critic, John Churton Collins. In a brief introduction to a selection from the *Pastime* ("his minor poems are best forgotten") published in 1880, he provides a remarkably balanced view of Hawes's poetry. He begins with a criticism of his style, which

has little of the fluency of Lydgate, and none of his vigour; none of the picturesqueness and brilliance which are characteristic of Chaucer and not less characteristic of Chaucer's Scotch disciples who were Hawes' contemporaries. The narrative . . . wants as a rule life and variety. The composition is often loose and feeble, the vocabulary is singularly limited, and bad taste is conspicuous in every canto.[59]

Yet for all this, Collins finds much to praise:

But Hawes, for all his faults, is a true poet. He has a sweet simplicity, a pensively gentle air, a subdued cheerfulness about him which have a strange charm at this distance of dissimilar time.[60]

He goes on to speak admiringly of Hawes's famous couplet, "For though the day be neuer so longe / At last the belles ryngeth to euensonge" (5479–80):

That couplet alone should suffice for immortality. We may claim also for this neglected poet complete originality at an age when English poetry at least had degenerated into mere translations, into feeble narratives, or into sickly imitations of Chaucer.[61]

Like Thomas Wright, Collins places Hawes as a transitional figure. The *Pastime* "marks with singular precision a great epoch in our literature. It was the last expiring echo of Mediaevalism; it is the first articulate prophecy of the Renaissance." For Collins, Hawes is preeminently a poet to be rescued from "the injustice which all his critics have inexplicably done him."[62]

Twentieth-century criticism, when it has considered Hawes at all, has tended to continue to see him in nineteenth-century terms. The standard surveys by Murison and Berdan exemplify this. Murison, writing in the *Cambridge History of English Literature* (1917), is not unsympathetic, especially to the *Pastime of Pleasure,* but largely sees Hawes as a transitional figure, struggling to throw off the trammels of medievalism and speak with an authentic voice, but handicapped by his metrical ineptitude.[63] Berdan, in his *Early Tudor Poetry* (1920) is not so positive. Much of Hawes's work he dismisses as "dull, incoherent, verbose." Once again, he is seen as a poet of the transition "the gate between medievalism and the Renaissance."[64]

Such views are not altogether surprising when one reflects that we still lack a proper critical edition of the *Pastime of Pleasure,* Hawes's major poem. It has been edited in this century by W. E. Mead for the Early English Text Society in 1928. But his edition is simply a verbatim reprint of the 1517 de Worde one, complete with misprints, and perfunctory commentary. It was not until 1974 that the rest of Hawes's poems were available in a reasonably edited form in the *Minor Poems*—including the first edition of the *Comfort of Lovers* for over 450 years.

It is hardly surprising therefore that most comment on Hawes during the past fifty years has been in the form of either specialist scholarly notes or brief critical dismissals. There are few significant exceptions to such tendencies. One is perhaps W. H. Auden, who was sufficiently inspired once to contemplate "a long poem . . . a very long dream sequence something like the *Roman de la Rose,* or the *Hous of Fame* or *The Pastime of Pleasure*."[65] But the poem, alas, remained uncompleted, and all that remains of it shows none of Hawes's influence.

Another sympathetic reader was C. S. Lewis, who wrote admiringly, as we have seen, of the *Example of Virtue* and the *Pastime of Pleasure* in *The Allegory of Love* (1936) and later offered a brief but trenchant defense of Hawes in his volume *English Literature in the Sixteenth Century* (1954) for the Oxford History of English Literature series:

Mrs. Browning claimed for him "true poetic faculty," but "faculty" seems to me exactly the wrong word. Faculty was what he lacked; there was more and better poetry in him than he could express. The adventurousness, the wonder, and the devout solemnity of his allegorical stories gleam fitfully through his broken backed metre and dull excursions into the seven liberal arts. There is a certain genuinely medieval fineness and simplicity about his mind if not about his art. . . . His failure excites sympathy rather than contempt.[66]

One can detect here echoes of the earlier criticism of Browning, Morley, and Saintsbury, of the view of Hawes as a potential poet. Lewis has been the most friendly of Hawes's twentieth-century critics, and he has stood virtually alone among such critics in his consistent championing of Hawes's achievement as a limited but genuine one.

Achievement

A couple of tendencies can be seen running through critical commentary on Hawes's poetry from the latter part of the nineteenth century onward. In the first place, there has been general criticism of his metrics—the view first enunciated by Henry Morley that Hawes was "held by his ears when he was dipped in Helicon." This has become a commonplace of criticism of Hawes's verse.

It is beyond dispute that Hawes's versification is erratic. His intermittently successful metrical effects, as in the *Conversion of Swearers*, have to be set against his halting rhyme royal and clattering couplets. But having conceded this, any accusation of metrical ineptitude on Hawes's part needs some qualification; needs to be set clearly in perspective. It is relevant here to recall that it is possible to overestimate his degree of metrical incompetence when seen in relation to other contemporary poets. Fitzroy Pyle, in an interesting study, has argued that the *Pastime of Pleasure* "shows a greater approach to metrical consistency than most fifteenth-century works in this kind [of metre] . . . . I should say that 60 per cent of the lines are ten-syllabled heroics and a larger proportion five-accented."[67] Later he contends that "there is a greater proportion of impeccable ten-syllabled heroics in the *Pastime of Pleasure* than in perhaps any other poem written in the conventional 'mingled' mode."[68] Ian Robinson has also briefly affirmed—and disapproved of—what he terms Hawes's "deadly balanced pentameters," which he feels constitute a slavish imitation of Lydgate's own metrical regularity.[69] But, in fact, Mead's demonstration of the variation and flexibility of Hawes's pentameter suggests that the degree of opprobrium his meter has received is excessive.[70] While his control lacks absolute confidence and can be maladroit, it would seem that it was probably better than that of any post-Lydgate poet in its use of rhyme royal.

The other general notion about Hawes is harder to respond to since it is less clearly defined. This is the idea that he is a "potential poet," one whose conceptions are not generally matched by his execution. This idea has been enunciated by a number of critics, most notably by C. S. Lewis. Once again, it has an element of justice. There is, at times, a gap that can become an unbridgeable abyss between intention and execution in Hawes's poetry. We often find an accumulation of heterogeneous materials, drawn from different modes and genres, which are placed in conjunctions which appear highly perplexing for a modern reader, in particular because of the narrative discontinuities these occasion. The intrusion of the Seven Liberal Arts into the *Pastime of Pleasure,* the extended debate in the first half of the *Example of Virtue,* and the episode of the three mirrors in the *Comfort of Lovers* are all instances where Hawes's use of such materials leaves a modern reader at best uncertain of his bearings, if not wholly confused.

I have tried to suggest in my accounts of particular poems, notably the *Pastime of Pleasure,* that Hawes does have much more of a controlling sense in his use of such materials than may be immediately apparent. But such a controlling sense is not consistently apparent even to the most sympathetic attempt to explicate his works, and there remain aspects, of varying importance, that resist all but the most tentative of conjectures. To this extent it is valid to see Hawes as a potential poet, all of whose works are, to a greater or lesser degree, flawed by failures or execution. But such a view, however valid, is not by any means the whole story.

In the first place, it is worth stressing that Hawes is remarkably interesting as a transitional poet, existing in a relationship both to earlier, medieval English traditions of verse writing and also a part of a milieu in which such traditions were being reworked or superseded. The designation "transitional" has become something of a cliché with respect to English poetry of the fifteenth and early sixteenth centuries, a way of accepting and justifying its badness rather than seeking its merits. But in Hawes's case the term does have a validity that can, properly applied, afford some insight into his poetic achievement.

Thus we perceive in his work a use of medieval poetic traditions and resources. He looks to medieval allegories of love, to the exposition of the Seven Liberal Arts, and to such conventional topics as the Nine Worthies, the Seven Deadly Sins, and complaints against swearers for his poetic materials. He draws in style and attitude from his mentor Lydgate. And he shows a generalized consciousness of earlier literary traditions as providing models for his own activities.

Often, however, his themes seek to deploy these debts to medieval tradition in new ways. For example, his stress on pragmatic, practical education for the nobility in the *Pastime of Pleasure* has been seen as "one of the most original" of his achievements, giving "a fundamentally medieval tradition a pecularly Renaissance twist."[71] Similarly, his discussions of aspects of rhetoric in the same poem break new ground and anticipate directions in Renaissance thought, as we have seen.[72]

But in much broader ways his use of his medieval poetic resources is strikingly innovative. As I have sought to show, much of his poetry appears to draw its impetus from contemporary events and circumstances. His shorter poems, the *Conversion of Swearers* and *A Joyful Meditation,* are clearly personal responses to contemporary circumstances or events. *The Example of Virtue* and *Pastime of Pleasure* seem to be controlled to a greater or lesser extent by attempts to make their materials applicable to contemporary circumstances. The *Comfort of Lovers* remains so obscure for modern readers because of its texture of occasional and autobiographical allusiveness.

What we find is that Hawes is at pains to maintain, both overtly and allegorically, a connection between the content of his writings and the contemporary, courtly world of which he was a part. His cumbersome medieval poetic resources are given a new orientation, if not a new impetus. The observation of his editors about the *Comfort of Lovers* has a wider applicability than they suggest:

Just as the general atmosphere of Tudor England led him to move from spiritual to secular allegory so his personal position forced him to try to extend the traditional form into new areas, to make it do new things.[73]

Two of these "new things" are particularly important. The first is Hawes's evident sense of the role of the poet, particularly within a courtly society. He sees his function clearly as an admonitory, didactic one. The role of the poet becomes that of critic, guide, and reformer, providing more or less under the veil of allegory a commentary on contemporary conduct, particularly among the ruling class. He provides not so much a series of injunctions on proper conduct as a series of allegorical homilies that modulate between the general and the particular but always retain at least some broad applicability to the circumstances of Hawes's court circle and especially to Henry VII. The willingness to give his poetry such a contemporary applicability indicates a degree of personal courage and integrity when one considers the degree to which personal well-being, prospects of advancement, and even life itself were, in Hawes's case, dependent upon royal favor. Hawes's poetry often reflects the attempt to walk a narrow line between offending his betters and articulating principles and beliefs in accord with his notions of moral integrity.

The delicacy of his position provides a partial justification for the cumbersomeness of much of his poetry. The lumbering allegorical machinery he employs does seek to make traditional poetic forms do new things. Allegory becomes not simply didactic, but admonitory, moving from generalized sentiousness to particular application. And at the same time Hawes's frequent expressions of admiration for literary tradition—Chaucer, Gower, and especially Lydgate—provide a justification for his choice of forms. Thus he is enabled to preserve a delicate balance between discretion and admonition.

It is, however, the fact of his situation that focuses the other important "new thing" in Hawes's poetry. For Hawes remains clearly very conscious of his own situation vis-à-vis the court circle in relation to what he is trying to say in his poetry. This consciousness makes him arguably the first English poet to attempt, on any scale, to turn autobiography into the subject matter of his poetry.[74] This is particularly evident in his final, most cryptic work. *The Comfort of Lovers,* although his sense of a relationship between his writings and his personal identity is evident in some of his other poems. But in the *Comfort* we see Hawes striking a new vein of personal complaint that is unusual if not unprecedented in English verse. It has "a strong sense of personal involvement, even urgency"[75] and seeks to give poetic form to harrowing personal experience. If the poem itself cannot be adjudged a success—it remains too inaccessible and the relationship between form and content too unclear—it does suggest a way in which Hawes was capable of channeling his poetic concerns in new ways. The problem is, once again, the failure in execution of an unusual conception.

A similar problem dogs another aspect of Hawes's innovativeness. He is the first English poet to combine allegory and romance, as he does in both the *Example of Virtue* and *Pastime of Pleasure*. Once again, we see him as an anticipator of modes of verse writing which were, in more skillful hands, to be explored with a fuller sense of their potential. His poems are in this respect curiously anticipatory analogues of Spenser's *Faerie Queene*. But Hawes's use of romance motifs is never integrated into a coherent design with his allegorical concerns as Spenser's is. For the quest is never a central aspect of such concerns. He remains much more interested in his static, allegorical, expository set pieces than in any combination of allegory and romance that would yield incremental or evolving significations for his poem. His essentially medieval sensibility severely circumscribes the potential of his innovative technique.

In at least one other respect Hawes can be seen as a harbinger of the Renaissance. This is his sense of the potentially fruitful relationship between words and images in his poetry. As I suggested in chapter 1, there were evidently careful, highly deliberate efforts made by Hawes and his publisher de Worde to insure a significant correlation between text and woodcut in the *Example of Virtue* and the *Pastime of Pleasure*. They evidently perceived the complementary nature of the two forms and sought to exploit this perception. Such curious innovativeness can be seen as an extension of the expository, didactic element in Hawes's poetry, prompting him to seek to have rendered in dramatic, visual terms what he was trying to express in his verse. In this respect he anticipates the emblem writers of the later sixteenth and seventeenth centuries, who rediscovered and redeveloped what Hawes had earlier perceived about the fruitful links between word and image.

In such respects it is possible to claim Hawes as an innovator, an anticipator of new and fruitful developments in English literary history. But it is not possible to claim any direct influence on later and/or more gifted writers except in the limited terms I have indicated. Hawes constitutes virtually an historical dead end. Later writers were to proceed by different routes to arrive at the point he had reached and then perceive a clear direction forward.

The nature of Hawes's failure becomes clearer when contrasted with the work of his contemporary or near contemporary fellow poets. He lacks any evident inspiration from humanist or classical writings of the sort that can be found in the poems of Wyatt or Surrey in, for example, the former's translations from Petrarch or the latter's rendering of Vergil's *Aeneid.* Even such a limited poet as Alexander Barclay proved sufficiently sensitive to the new cultural climate to produce the first English eclogues. But Hawes set his face firmly against such tendencies, preferring to seek his inspiration in the native traditions of verse writing, looking back to the triumvirate of Chaucer, Gower, and Lydgate, and drawing on an ill-digested stock of conventional formulae and topics. He embodies a cultural last stand, remaining resolutely parochial at a time when more astute and gifted writers were already sniffing the winds of change.

His style is equally limited. It draws once more, in language and technique, upon the past: his erratic rhyme royal, his leaden couplets, his stock phrases all bespeak lessons learned diligently from his predecessors, but learned without understanding. A comparison with his fellow courtier John Skelton is relevant here. Both began their poetic careers in about the same relationship to earlier poetic traditions. Skelton's first major poem, *The Bouge of Court,* was a dream allegory in rhyme royal. But whereas Hawes never really moved stylistically beyond this, we see Skelton advancing to develop new poetic techniques, such as his use of Skeltonics, which enabled him to refine characteristically medieval forms like complaint and satire to give them new vitality and urgency. Hawes's own complaints remain stifled by their allegorical apparatus much of the time, even though he seems to care as urgently as Skelton about aspects of the contemporary political scene and court life. Skelton can find new and appropriate poetic modes for voicing his concerns. Hawes cannot.

But Hawes is not to be disparaged or ignored on these grounds. Rather, he is worth reading because he reveals the problems of an aspiring poet in early Renaissance England. We see how a commitment to earlier modes and styles of verse writing serves, in effect, to thwart the full expression of a genuine poetic talent. If Hawes's execution does not match his conception, then the reasons why this is so tell us a great deal about the cultural and social situation of Hawes's time and place.

Hawes, then, is an interesting minor poet. He is of less significance, historically or intrinsically, than his contemporaries Skelton or Wyatt.

But he is still worth our attention, for he marks a watershed, the last fling of an outmoded medieval poetic, which he was already reshaping to serve new purposes and occasions. He did not live to complete this task. But he has left, particularly in his most important poem, *The Pastime of Pleasure,* and his most enigmatic, *The Comfort of Lovers,* abundant evidence to justify his claims to serious, sympathetic response from modern readers.

Notes and References

Chapter One

1. John Bale, *Scriptorum Illustrium Maioris Brytanniae* (Basle, 1557), p. 632. (I have translated Bale's Latin.)

2. See *Calendar of Close Rolls . . . Henry VII* (London, HMSO, 1963), 2:257, item 683.

3. See A. B. Emden, *A Biographical Register of the University of Oxford to A. D. 1500* (Oxford, 1957), 2:888–89.

4. This document was first printed by John Payne Collier in his *History of English Dramatic Poetry* (1831), 1:48. It is reprinted, together with other notices of Hawes in the article on him in the *Dictionary of National Biography*.

5. The facts are set out in G. S. Humphreys, "Stephen Hawes" (M.A. thesis, University of London, 1928), p. 66.

6. See, for example, F. W. Gluck and A. Morgan, eds., *Stephen Hawes: The Minor Poems* (London, 1974), p. xxii, for discussion of such attributions. This edition will be used throughout for quotations from Hawes's *Example of Virtue, Conversion of Swearers, A Joyful Meditation,* and *Comfort of Lovers.* Hawes's *Pastime of Pleasure* will be cited from the edition of W. E. Mead (London, 1928). I have generally omitted virgules in the middle of lines when quoting from these two editions and I have occasionally emended the text when a reading seems incorrect.

7. See, for example, W. Murison, "Stephen Hawes," in *The Cambridge History of English Literature* (Cambridge, 1917), 2:255.

8. For recent helpful discussion of the role of the Groom of the Privy Chamber and especially of his literary significance see R. F. Green, *Poets and Princepleasers* (Toronto: University of Toronto Press, 1980), pp. 38–70.

9. The standard discussion of Henry's life and career is S. B. Chrimes, *Henry VII* (London: Eyre Methuen, 1972), to which this paragraph is indebted.

10. For the most recent account of André see G. Kipling, *The Triumph of Honour* (The Hague: Leiden University Press, 1977), pp. 16–20.

11. On English and Cornish see S. Anglo, *Spectacle, Pageantry and Early Tudor Policy* (Oxford: Clarendon Press, 1969), pp. 117–21 and Kipling, *Triumph,* esp. pp. 100–15, 175–77.

12. The best biographies of Skelton are by W. Nelson, *John Skelton, Laureate* (New York: Columbia University Press, 1939), and H. L. R. Edwards, *Skelton* (London: Jonathon Cape, 1949).

13. The best biography of Barclay is still that by T. H. Jamieson in the Introduction to his edition of *The Ship of Fools* (Edinburgh, 1874).

14. On this see R. S. Kinsman, "A Skelton Reference c. 1510," *Notes & Queries* 205 (1960):210–11.

15. On Margaret see especially W. E. A. Axon, "The Lady Margaret as a Lover of Literature," *Library,* n.s. 8(1907):34–41.

16. N. F. Blake, "Wynken de Worde: The Later Years," *Gutenberg Jahrbuch* (1972), p. 134. This hypothesis gains a measure of support from the fact that her household included others who shared her interest in vernacluary literature. Her Clerk of Works, James Morice, is known to have owned copies of Chaucer, Gower, Rolle, and Lydgate, for example; see J. C. T. Oates, "'English Bokes Concernyng to James Morice,'" *Transactions of the Cambridge Bibliographical Society* 3, pt. 2 (1960):124–32.

17. She owned copies of Lydgate's *Troy Book* and *Fall of Princes* (Axon, 41).

18. See further on this in my *John Skelton: The Critical Heritage* (London: Routledge and Kegan Paul, 1981), pp. 3–8.

19. This suggestion was first made by I. A. Gordon, *Times Literary Supplement,* 15 November 1934.

20. See *The Poetical Works of John Skelton,* ed. Alexander Dyce (1843; reprint ed., New York: AMS Press, 1965), 1:119, line 36.

21. See *Minor Poems,* pp. 160–62.

22. See further R. Weiss, *Humanism in England during the Fifteenth Century,* 2d ed. (Oxford: Blackwell, 1957).

23. *The Correspondence of Erasmus,* trans. R. A. B. Mynors and D. F. S. Thomson (Toronto: University of Toronto Press, 1974–), 1:235–36.

24. On humanism and Henry VII's court see Nelson, *John Skelton,* pp. 4–39.

25. This has been argued by C. F. Bühler, "'Kynge Melyzyus' and *The Pastime of Pleasure,*" *Review of English Studies* 10 (1934):438–41.

26. See C. W. Lemmi, "The Influence of Boccaccio on Hawes's *Pastime of Pleasure,*" *Review of English Studies* 5 (1929):195–98.

27. See *Lord Morley's Tryumphes of Fraunces Petrarcke,* ed. D. D. Carnicelli (Cambridge, Mass.: Harvard University Press, 1971), pp. 49–52.

28. See below, chapter 2, and A. B. Ferguson, *The Indian Summer of English Chivalry* (Durham, N.C., 1960), pp. 66–68.

29. See Mead's introduction to the *Pastime,* esp. p. lxxviii, for discussion of these questions.

30. Anthony à Wood, *Athenae Oxonienses,* 1691–92, 3d ed. (1813–20), 1:cols. 9–10.

31. The standard account of Lydgate is D. Pearsall, *John Lydgate* (London: Routledge & Kegan Paul, 1970).

32. See J. M. Berdan, *Early Tudor Poetry* (New York: Macmillan, 1920), p. 139.

33. The best account of the term is in J. Norton Smith, ed., *John Lydgate: Poems* (Oxford: Clarendon Press, 1966), pp. 192–95.

34. See Berdan, *Early Tudor Poetry,* p. 140.

35. *Minor Poems,* p. xxxiii.

36. Some of these are given in the notes to the standard edition of the *Pastime* and the *Minor Poems.*

37. *The Minor Poems of John Lydgate,* ed. H. N. MacCracken (London: Oxford University Press, 1934), 2:832.

38. Lydgate, *Fall of Princes,* ed. H. Bergen (London: Oxford University Press, 1924–27), 2:4432–38.

39. The best account is N. F. Blake, "Wynkyn de Worde: The Early Years," *Gutenberg Jahrbuch* (1971), pp. 62–69 and "Wynkyn de Worde: The Later Years," *Gutenberg Jahrbuch* (1972), pp. 128–38.

40. Ibid., p. 134.

41. See "Poet and Printer in Sixteenth Century England: Stephen Hawes and Wynkyn de Worde," *Gutenberg Jahrbuch* (1980), pp. 82–88. It is not possible to include woodcuts here, but most are printed in the editions of Hawes by Mead and Gluck and Morgan of the *Pastime* and *Minor Poems,* respectively. All woodcuts in the early editions of Hawes poems appear in the facsimile edition of *The Works of Stephen Hawes,* with an introduction by F. J. Spang (Delmar, N.Y., 1975).

42. For discussion of this question see the Introduction to my *John Skelton: The Critical Heritage,* pp. 4–5, 7–8.

43. There are a few scattered manuscript extracts from Hawes's poems, but these seem to have postdated the printed editions; see below, chap. 4.

Chapter Two

1. E. P. Hammond, *English Verse between Chaucer and Surrey* (Durham, N.C.: Duke University Press, 1927), p. 269, argues for the influence of Chaucer's *Troilus and Criseyde* on one or two passages; Mead in his edition of the *Pastime* notes some verbal echoes (see above and chap. 1, fn. 29).

2. Murison, in his chapter on Hawes in the *Cambridge History of English Literature,* 2:262, argues that "Gower's Confessio provides the fabliaux about

Aristotle and Vergil" used in the Godfrey Gobelive episode; but Gower's references are too slight to provide any basis.

3. R. S. Crane, *The Vogue of Medieval Chivalric Romance during the English Renaissance* (Menasha: University of Pennsylvania, 1919), p. 10.

4. E. C. Knowlton, "Nature in Middle English," *Journal of English and Germanic Philology* 20 (1921):200–207.

5. "He [Lydgate] fayned also the court of sapyence" (1357).

6. W. Wells, "Stephen Hawes and *The Court of Sapience*," *Review of English Studies* 6 (1930):284–94.

7. Hammond, *English Verse*, p. 270.

8. See S. C. Chew, *The Pilgrimage of Life* (New Haven, 1962).

9. See S. Wenzel, "The Pilgrimage of Life as a Late Medieval Genre," *Mediaeval Studies* 35 (1973):369–88.

10. Ibid., pp. 373–74, for discussion of the *Pelerinage.*

11. Edited as *The Pilgrimage of the Life of Man* by F. J. Furnivall and K. B. Locock, 3 vols. (London, 1899–1904).

12. On this tradition see Chew, *Pilgrimage of Life*, pp. 140–41.

13. See M. W. Bloomfield, *The Seven Deadly Sins* (East Lansing, Mich., 1952), p. 240.

14. Chew, *Pilgrimage of Life*, p. 176.

15. Ibid., pp. 186–88, for discussion of Cupid's arrows.

16. C. S. Lewis, *The Allegory of Love* (London, 1936), p. 280.

17. On the background of the Seven Liberal Arts see E. R. Curtius, *European Literature in the Latin Middle Ages* (New York: Pantheon Books, 1953), pp. 36–42.

18. Chew, *Pilgrimage of Life*, p. 197, observes that this separation is "noteworthy."

19. For extensive discussion of this question see W. S. Howells, *Logic and Rhetoric in England, 1500–1700* (Princeton, 1956), pp. 81–88.

20. See Frances Yates, *The Art of Memory* (London: Routledge & Kegan Paul, 1966), p. 260.

21. Ferguson, *Indian Summer*, p. 211 (in a discussion of this passage).

22. Ibid., pp. 67–68, notes that "Hawes refers repeatedly to the practical application of the liberal arts, especially that of rhetoric."

23. On the tradition of Vergil the magician as it applies to this passage see J. W. Spargo, *Virgil the Necromancer* (Cambridge, Mass., 1934), p. 54.

24. See F. L. Utley, *The Crooked Rib* (Columbus: Ohio State University Press, 1944), pp. 102, 142, 297–98, 308–9.

25. J. A. Bennett, *The Parlement of Foules: An Interpretation* (Oxford: Clarendon Press, 1957), pp. 107–33.

26. Lines 4368–4416, 4802–57, 5117–51.

27. See Carnicelli, *Lord Morley's Tryumphes,* pp. 48–52, and R. Coogan, "Petrarch's *Trionfi* and the English Renaissance," *Studies in Philology* 67 (1970):306–27.

28. See Bloomfield, *Seven Deadly Sins,* passim.

29. Ibid., p. 240.

30. The best brief discussion of this tradition is in *The Parliament of the Three Ages,* ed. M. Y. Offord (London: Oxford University Press, 1959), pp. xl-xlii.

31. Lewis, *Allegory of Love,* p. 284.

32. Ibid., p. 285: "If the execution of this whole passage had been equal to the conception, it would have been among the great places of medieval poetry."

33. For examples see lines 409, 2009, 2559, 4938.

34. *Oxford English Dictionary,* s.v. "pastime," sb. 2.

35. See John N. King, "Allegorical Patterns in Stephen Hawes's *The Pastime of Pleasure,*" *Studies in the Literary Imagination* 11 (1978):59.

36. See further on Henry's fiscal policies, especially during his later years, Chrimes, *Henry VII,* pp. 216–17, and the references cited there; and J. R. Lander, *Crown and Nobility, 1450–1509* (Montreal: McGill-Queen's University Press, 1976), pp. 267–300 *passim.*

37. Polydore Vergil, *Historia Anglicana,* ed. D. Hay (London: Camden Society, 1950), p. 129.

38. C. S. Lewis, *English Literature in the Sixteenth Century Excluding Drama* (London, 1954), p. 218.

39. D. Pearsall, *Old English and Middle English Poetry* (London, 1977), p. 267, describes his verse as "a labouring pentameter on the verge always of breakdown."

40. Mead, Introduction to his edition of *Pastime of Pleasure,* xciv–ix.

41. Ibid., p. civ.

42. For examples, see ibid., pp. cviii, cx–xi.

43. A number of these are noted in the Commentary on the *Example of Virtue* in *Minor Poems.*

44. For a succinct critique of Hawes's style, see G. S. Fraser, "Skelton and the Dignity of Poetry," *Adelphi* 13 (1936):154–55.

45. See B. J. Whiting, *Proverbs, Sentences and Proverbial Phrases from English Writings Mainly before 1500* (Cambridge, Mass.: Harvard University Press, 1968), items D31, D40, and E80, which list the precedents for Hawes's lines in this stanza.

46. Pearsall, *Old English,* p. 267.

Chapter Three

1. See, for example, Chew, *Pilgrimage of Life,* pp. 204–6, and Wenzel, "Pilgrimage of Life," pp. 377–79.

2. See *Minor Poems,* pp. 125–26, 131.

3. Ibid., p. xlii.

4. Ibid., p. 124.

5. See Wells, "Stephen Hawes," pp. 184–94.

6. For example, those in lines 59, 146–47, 574, 1695.

7. Lewis, *Allegory of Love,* p. 286.

8. On this Act see Chrimes, *Henry VII,* p. 236.

9. See Lewis, *Allegory of Love,* pp. 285–86, to which this paragraph is greatly indebted.

10. For details see A. Morgan, "The Conuercyon of Swerers: Another Edition," *Library* 5th series, 24 (1969):44–50.

11. R. Woolf, *The English Religious Lyric in the Middle Ages* (Oxford, 1968), pp. 395–400.

12. Ibid., p. 399.

13. I use the definition in Pearsall, *Old English,* p. 289.

14. For example, Herbert's "Easter Wings," where the lines of verse form the shape of a pair of wings.

15. See Margaret Church, "The First English Pattern Poems," *PMLA* 61 (1946):637–38 and the edition by R. T. Davies in his *Medieval English Lyrics* (London: Faber & Faber, 1963), no. 152 and p. 360.

16. See P. J. Frankis, "The Syllabic Value of Final '-es' in English Versification about 1500," *Notes & Queries* 212 (1967):11–12.

17. Berdan observes (pp. 88–89) that "[it] is chiefly interesting for the complete reversal of one of his prophecies, that expressed in 155–61 that Henry VIII will be the Church's 'shelde from all aduersytee.' "

18. *The Latin Epigrams of Thomas More,* ed. L. Bradner and C. A. Lynch (Chicago: University of Chicago Press, 1953), p. 139.

19. See, e.g., the account in the *Great Chronicle of London,* ed. A. H. Thomas and I. D. Thornley (London: privately printed, 1938), pp. 338–39.

20. The discussion of this passage in *Minor Poems,* p. 154, is confused and inaccurate; it is there stated that the *Pastime of Pleasure* was composed in 1506/7 (actually between August 1505 and August 1506) and the *Comfort of Lovers* in 1510 (actually between April 1510 and April 1511). This seems to be prompted by a desire to make the chronology of Hawes's works fit this mention of "thre yeres."

21. The best discussion of lines 134–40 is a letter by P. Parker, "Stephen Hawes," in the *Times Literary Supplement,* 21 June 1928, p. 468. I am indebted to Mr. Parker's account (which is not noted by the editors of *Minor Poems*).

22. This notion is advanced in *Minor Poems,* p. 154.

23. For a discussion of Skelton's possible significance in the *Comfort of Lovers,* see *Minor Poems,* pp. 160–62.

24. Some of these are noted in the Commentary on the poem in *Minor Poems,* pp. 152–62 passim.

25. Cf. ibid., p. 157; the form "prepudence" does not appear in the *Oxford English Dictionary;* the form "prepense" to which I take it to be related is used by Hawes in the *Pastime of Pleasure* and is apparently his neologism, where it means "to plan, devise or contrive beforehand" (s.v. "prepense," *v. Obs.* 1).

26. See the discussion of the term in *Minor Poems,* pp. 127–28.

27. See below, chapter 4.

28. *Minor Poems,* p. xlvi.

Chapter Four

1. For an account of this disorder see Mead's edition of the *Pastime,* p. xxx.

2. All these variants are noted in the edition of the *Minor Poems* by Gluck and Morgan, but they make no attempt to account for them.

3. See, for example, R. W. Mitchner, "Wynkyn de Worde's Use of the Plimpton Manuscript of *De Proprietatibus Rerum,*" *Library* 5th ser., no. 6 (1951), pp. 7–18.

4. I have quoted from the slightly modernized text in *The Dunbar Anthology,* ed. E. Arber (London, 1901), p. 193.

5. Chaucer, *The assemble of foules* (1530), A1ˇ.

6. See further on this point my note "An Allusion to Stephen Hawes, c. 1530," *Notes & Queries* 224 (1979):397.

7. H. R. Plomer, "An Inventory of Wynkyn de Worde's House 'The Sun in Fleet Street' in 1553," *Library* 3rd ser., no. 6 (1915), p. 232.

8. Quoted in Mead's edition of the *Pastime,* pp. xxxi, xxxiii.

9. See A. G. Watson, *The Manuscripts of Henry Savile of Banke* (London: Oxford University Press, 1969), who records among a list of the contents of Savile's library in the early seventeenth century a work described as "Liber qui vocatur Lusus delitiae de septem sientiis, compositus per Stephanum Hawes, verso anglico" (64).

10. No. 2318 in C. Brown and R. H. Robbins *Index of Middle English Verse* (New York: Index Society, 1943).

11. These poems are all printed by F. M. Padelford and A. R. Benham, "The Songs in Manuscript Rawlinson C. 813," *Anglia* 31 (1908):309–27; the poems containing Hawes material are nos. 13, 14, 15, 16, and 48.

12. Poem no. 13; see, e.g., *Pastime,* 4086: "Of Septembre the two and twenty day" becomes in Rawlinson "Aprell the nyen and twenty day." I owe

this point to Dr. Katherine Power, who is engaged in working on an edition of this manuscript.

13. See *Minor Poems,* p. xxi, for full details.

14. No. 4216 in the *Index of Middle English Verse.*

15. *Minor Poems,* pp. xxi–ii.

16. Arber, *Dunbar Anthology,* p. 204.

17. Hammond, *English Verse between Chaucer and Surrey,* p. 287.

18. See further my "Nevill's *Castle of Pleasure* and Stephen Hawes," *Notes & Queries* 226 (1981):487.

19. See R. Southall, *The Courtly Maker* (Oxford: Blackwell, 1964), pp. 39–40.

20. See I. Lancashire, ed., *Two Tudor Interludes: The Interludes of Youth and Hickscorner* (Manchester: Manchester University Press, 1980), pp. 39–40.

21. Gerard Leigh, *The Accedens of Armoury* (1560), ff. 207–11.

22. See further Marie Axton, "Robert Dudley and the Inner Temple Revels," *Historical Journal* 13 (1970):365–78; H. Schroeder, "Gerard Leigh, Stephen Hawes, and the Nine Worthies," *Notes & Queries* 222 (1977):46–48; D. S. Bland, "Gerard Leigh and Stephen Hawes," *Notes & Queries* 222 (1977):497; for an attempted reconstruction of Broke's masque, which fails fully to grasp Hawes's influence, see D. S. Bland, "Arthur Broke's *Masque of Beauty and Desire:* A Reconstruction," *Research Opportunities in Renaissance Drama* 19 (1976):49–56.

23. Leigh, *The Accedens of Armoury,* f. 207.

24. Ibid., f. 211.

25. Ibid.

26. Raphael Holinshed, *Chronicles of England, Scotland and Ireland* (London, 1808), 3:543.

27. The most extensive discussion of the question of the relationship between Hawes and Spenser is in *The Works of Edmund Spenser,* ed. E. Greenlaw et al. (Baltimore: The Johns Hopkins Press, 1932), 1:414–18. It is erroneously stated there that the tradition that Hawes was a source for the *Faerie Queene* derives from Thomas Warton's *History of English Poetry* (1778). Although Warton notes *stylistic* similarities between the two works, the first person to suggest the *Pastime* as a source for Spenser seems to have been Elizabeth Barrett Browning.

28. C. S. Lewis, *Studies in Medieval and Renaissance Literature* (Cambridge: At the University Press, 1966), pp. 130–31.

29. See Murison, "Stephen Hawes," pp. 266–68, and *The Works of Edmund Spenser,* 1:416–17, for these parallels.

30. Anthony à Wood, *Athenae Oxonienses,* ed. P. Bliss (London, 1813), cols. 9–10.

31. See *A Catalogue of a portion of the Remaining Library of George Mason* (London, 1799), 4:21, lots 275 and 276.

32. See H. Sellers, "Two Poems by Hawes and an Early Medical Tract," *British Museum Quarterly* 13 (1939):7–8.

33. See A. N. L. Munby, ed., *Sale Catalogues of Libraries of Eminent Persons: Poets and Men of Letters* (London: Mansell, 1971), 2:19; in the original sale on 29 November 1845, this copy was lot 775 and was described as having "MS. Notes and Corrections by Gray."

34. See D. Fairer, "The Origins of Warton's History of English Poetry," *Review of English Studies,* n.s. 32 (1981):37–63, for numerous expressions of his interest in Hawes among his manuscript collections.

35. Thomas Warton, *Observations on the Fairy Queen of Spenser,* 2d ed. (London, 1762), 2:105–6.

36. Thomas Warton, *History of English Poetry,* first edition (London, 1778).

37. Ibid., p. 210.

38. Ibid., p. 219.

39. Ibid., p. 236.

40. *The Correspondence of Thomas Percy and Thomas Warton,* ed. M. G. Robinson and Leah Dennis (Baton Rouge: Louisiana State University Press, 1951), p. 70; there are other mentions by Percy of Hawes on pp. 66 and 98.

41. He included lines 344–417 from the *Pastime.*

42. J. B. Nichols, *Illustrations of the Literary History of the Eighteenth Century* (London, 1858), 8:344–45.

43. See "The Roxburghe Sale" in *Gentleman's Magazine,* August 1812, pp. 113–16.

44. T. Dibdin, *The Library Companion* (London, 1824), p. 647.

45. Ibid., pp. 665–66.

46. George Ellis, *Specimens of the Early English Poets* (London, 1801), 1:402–6.

47. *The Prose Works of Sir Walter Scott* (Edinburgh, 1835), 17:13.

48. Thomas Campbell, ed., *Specimens of the British Poets* (1819; new ed., Philadelphia, 1854), pp. 20–21.

49. Robert Southey, ed., *Select Works of the British Poets* (London: Longman's Hurst, Rees and Orme, 1831), p. 75.

50. The article originally appeared in the *Athenaeum* for 11 June 1842; I quote from the version included in *The Greek Christian Poets and the English Poets* (London, 1863), pp. 123–24.

51. *The Pastime of Pleasure,* ed. T. Wright (London, 1845), pp. v–vi.

52. *The Conversyon of Swearers [and] A Joyfull Medytacyon to All Englonde of the Coronacyon of Kynge Henry the Eyght,* ed. D. Laing (Edinburgh, 1865).

53. In *The Dunbar Anthology* (London: Henry Frowde, 1901), pp. 219–96.

54. Stopford Brooke, *English Literature* (London: Macmillan, 1880), p. 60.

55. Henry Morley, *English Writers* (London: Cassell & Co., 1891), 7:73.

56. George Saintsbury, *A History of English Prosody* (1908; reprint ed., New York, 1961), 2d ed., 1:291.

57. Ibid., 1:237.

58. George Saintsbury, *The Earlier Renaissance* (Edinburgh: William Blackwood, 1923), p. 232.

59. *The English Poets,* ed. T. H. Ward (London: Macmillan, 1880), 1:175–76. Collins's admiration for Hawes is evident elsewhere. In his later *Ephemera Critica* (London: Constable, 1901) he observes: "what a singularly interesting poem, intrinsically and historically, the *Pastime of Pleasure* really is" (198) and describes it as "memorable alike both for the preciseness with which it marks the transition from the poetry of medievalism to that of the Renaissance, for its probable influence on Spenser, and for its intrinsic claims, its pathos, its picturesqueness, and its sweet and plaintive music" (200).

60. Ibid., 1:176.

61. Ibid.

62. Ibid., 1:176–77.

63. Murison, *Cambridge History of English Literature,* 2:254–71.

64. Berdan, *Early Tudor Poetry,* p. 84.

65. See Lucy S. McDiarmid, "W. H. Auden's 'In the Year of My Youth. . .,'" *Review of English Studies,* n.s. 29 (1978):267.

66. Lewis, *English Literature in the Sixteenth Century,* p. 128.

67. Fitzroy Pyle, "The Barbarous Metre of Barclay," *Modern Language Review* 32 (1937):355, note 1.

68. Ibid., p. 373.

69. Ian Robinson, *Chaucer's Prosody* (Cambridge: At the University Press, 1971), p. 215.

70. Mead, Introduction to his edition of *Pastime of Pleasure,* pp. xcii–ix.

71. Ferguson, *Indian Summer,* p. 67.

72. Howells, *Logic and Rhetoric in England,* pp. 81–88.

73. *Minor Poems,* p. xlvi.

74. It has been claimed that earlier English poets, notably Chaucer, Langland, and Hoccleve, reflected autobiographical experience in their poetry; but see G. Kane, *The Autobiographical Fallacy in Chaucer and Langland* (London: Athlone Press, 1965), and (on Hoccleve), P. B. R. Doob, *Nebuchadnezzar's Children* (New Haven: Yale University Press, 1974), pp. 208–31.

75. *Minor Poems,* p. xliv.

Selected Bibliography

PRIMARY SOURCES

1. Early Editions (listed chronologically)

The Example of Virtue. London, 1509. Printed by de Worde. On bibliographical grounds this can be dated before the *Pastime of Pleasure,* which was printed first on 11 January 1509.

[*The Pastime of Pleasure.*] London, 1509. Printed by de Worde. The first edition, extant only in a unique, imperfect copy, now in the British Library. It lacks lines 1–518, 2914–57, 3074–3172, 3463–3619, 3652–84, 3751–81, 3792–3820.

The Conversion of Swearers. London, 1509. Printed by de Worde, between April and June of that year. Reprinted, with variants, about 1510.

A Joyful Meditation. London, 1509. Printed by de Worde, presumably around the time of Henry VIII's coronation on 24 June.

The Comfort of Lovers. London, [ca. 1515]. Printed by de Worde.

The Pastime of Pleasure. London, 1517. Printed by de Worde. The earliest complete edition.

[*The Exampole of Virtue.*] [London, ca. 1520.] A single leaf, printed by de Worde.

The Example of Virtue. London, 1530. Printed by de Worde.

The Conversion of Swearers. London, 1530. Printed by John Butler.

The Conversion of Swearers. London, 1551. Printed by William Copland for Robert Toye.

The Pastime of Pleasure. London, 1554. Printed by John Wayland.

The Pastime of Pleasure. London, 1555. Printed by William Copland for Richard Tottel.

2. Manuscripts

Glasgow, University of Glasgow Hunterian MS 230, f. 246ᵛ. A single stanza (2542–48) from the *Pastime of Pleasure.*

London, British Library MS Harley 4294, f. 80. Lines 234–89 from the *Conversion of Swearers.*

Oxford, Bodleian Library MS Rawlinson C. 813. Several of the poems in this manuscript are largely made up of extracts from the *Pastime* (poems 13, 14, 15, and 48) and from the *Comfort of Lovers* (poem 16).

3. Major Modern Editions (listed chronologically under editor)

Southey, Robert. *Select Works of the British Poets from Chaucer to Jonson.* London: Longman's, Hurst, Rees and Orme, 1831. This includes the first edition of the *Pastime of Pleasure,* or indeed any of Hawes's works, since 1555. Southey reprinted Wayland's 1554 edition (76–126) with slight modernizations and omissions.

[Wright, Thomas.] *The Pastime of Pleasure,* London: Percy Society, 1845. An inaccurate and incomplete reprint of Tottel's 1555 edition.

Laing, David. *The Conversion of Swerers* [*and*] *A Joyful Medytacyon.* Edinburgh: Abbotsford Club, 1865. For the *Conversion* Laing used the ca. 1510 de Worde reprint, the Butler and Toye editions.

Arber, Edward. *The Dunbar Anthology: 1401–1508.* London: Henry Frowde, 1901. Contains slightly modernized text of the *Example of Virtue* (217–96).

Padelford, F. M., and **Benham, A. R.** "The Songs in Manuscript Rawlinson C. 813." *Anglia* 31 (1908):309–97. The texts printed here include several which include sixteenth-century adaptations of parts of Hawes's *Pastime of Pleasure* and/or *Comfort of Lovers*; see especially nos. 13, 14, 15, 16, and 48.

Hammond, Eleanor Prescott. *English Verse between Chaucer and Surrey.* Durham, N.C.: Duke University Press, 1927. Contains (271–86) lines 22–416, 470–518, 586–95, 715–819, 1156–76, 1310–1407, 1457–70, 4270–4507, from Wayland's 1554 edition. Contains some excellent commentary (487–95).

Mead, William Edward. *The Pastime of Pleasure.* London: Oxford University Press, 1928. Early English Text Society, original series, 173. The standard edition of the *Pastime,* based on de Worde's 1517 edition.

Scammell, G. V., and **Rogers, H. L.** "An Elegy on Henry VII." *Review of English Studies,* n.s. 8 (1957):167–70. Argues that this elegy might be by Hawes.

Gluck, Florence W., and **Morgan, Alice B.** *Stephen Hawes: The Minor Poems.* London: Oxford University Press, 1974. Early English Text Society, original series 271. The standard modern edition of Hawes's poems apart from the *Pastime.* It contains *The Example of Virtue* (based on de Worde's 1509 edition); *The Conversion of Swearers* (based on de Worde's 1509 edition); *A Joyful Meditation* (based on de Worde's 1509 edition); and *The Comfort of Lovers* (based on de Worde's [1515] edition). There are full collations of other early editions, notes, and an intelligent critical introduction.

Spang, Frank J. *The Works of Stephen Hawes.* Delmar, N.Y.: Scholar's Facsimiles & Reprints, 1975. A facsimile of all of Hawes's works, generally using the same editions as in the Mead and Gluck and Morgan editions; but for the *Conversion of Swearers* Spang uses de Worde's ca. 1510 reprint without noting that the final leaf is from Laing's 1865 edition. There is a brief introduction.

SECONDARY SOURCES

Atkins, J. W. H. *English Literary Criticism: The Medieval Phase.* London: Methuen, 1952. Discusses Hawes's theory of poetry.

Axton, Marie. "Robert Dudley and the Inner Temple Revels." *Historical Journal* 13 (1970):365–78. A discussion of the use of the *Pastime of Pleasure* as a source for the Inner Temple Revels of 1561 as reflected in Gerard Leigh's *Accedens of Armoury* (1562).

Bale, Bishop John. *Scriptorum Illustrium Maioris Brytanniae.* Basle, 1557. This work contains the first and only account of Hawes's life that possesses any authority.

Berdan, J. M. *Early Tudor Poetry.* New York: Macmillan, 1920. Contains the only attempt at an overall assessment of all Hawes's oeuvre. It sees him as attempting to shake off the limitations of medieval traditions and metrical ineptitude.

Bland, D. S. "Gerard Leigh and Stephen Hawes." *Notes & Queries* 222 (1977):497. A response to Schroeder's article (see below), discussing the failure of the 1561 Inner Temple Revels to include the description of the Nine Worthies from the *Pastime of Pleasure.*

Bloomfield, Morton W. *The Seven Deadly Sins.* East Lansing: Michigan State College Press, 1952. Contains a brief discussion of the presentation of the seven-metaled monster and the Seven Deadly Sins in the *Pastime of Pleasure.*

Bühler, Curt F. "'Kynge Melyzyus' and the *Pastime of Pleasure.*" *Review of English Studies* 10 (1934):438–41. A suggestion that the figure of King Melizius may have its origins in Pindar's third Isthmian Ode.

Burkart, Eugene A. *Stephen Hawes The Pastime of Pleasure. Critical Introduction to a Proposed New Edition.* London: Th. Wohlleben, 1899. The value of this work is seriously limited by its frequent references to notes for this projected edition which never appeared. It is also weakened by confusion and inaccuracy.

Carnicelli, D. D., ed. *Lord Morley's Tryumphes of Frances Petrarcke.* Cambridge, Mass.: Harvard University Press, 1971. Contains a discussion of the personifications of Fame, Time, and Eternity at the end of the *Pastime of Pleasure.*

Chew, S. C. *The Pilgrimage of Life*. New Haven: Yale University Press, 1962. A wide-ranging study of the literature and iconography of the pilgrimage of life which draws extensively on Hawes's *Example of Virtue* and *Pastime of Pleasure*.

Coogan, Robert. "Petrarch's Trionfi and the English Renaissance." *Studies in Philology* 67 (1970):306–27. Discusses the possible knowledge of the *Trionfi* evidenced by the end of the *Pastime of Pleasure*.

Edwards, A. S. G. "An Allusion to Stephen Hawes, c. 1530." *Notes & Queries* 224 (1979):397. Draws attention to a reference to Hawes by Robert Copland and links it to other indications of interest in Hawes within de Worde's circle.

————. "De Worde's Reprints of Stephen Hawes's Poems." *Gutenberg Jahrbuch* (1983). A discussion of de Worde's reprints of the *Pastime of Pleasure* and *Example of Virtue*.

————. "Nevill's *Castell of Pleasure* and Stephen Hawes," *Notes & Queries* 226 (1981):487. Discusses Nevill's use of the *Example of Virtue*.

————. "Poet and Printer in Sixteenth Century England: Stephen Hawes and Wynkyn de Worde." *Gutenberg Jahrbuch* (1980), pp. 82–88. Discusses the relationship between Hawes and de Worde.

Emden, A. B. *A Biographical Register of the University of Oxford to* A.D. *1500*. Oxford: Clarendon Press, 1957, 2:888–89. Notes that Hawes was possibly a commoner of Magdalen College, Oxford, in 1493.

Enkvist, Nils E. *The Seasons of the Year*. Helsinfors: Societas Scientiarun Fennica, 1957. Includes a discussion of Hawes's descriptions of nature in the *Pastime of Pleasure*, pointing to Lydgate's influence.

Ferguson, Arthur B. *The Indian Summer of English Chivalry*. Durham, N.C.: Duke University Press, 1960. An important discussion of Hawes as a "transitional" figure.

Frankis, P. J. "The Syllabic Value of Final -es in English Versification about 1500." *Notes & Queries* 212 (1967):11–12. A discussion of Hawes's *Conversion of Swearers*, showing that it is not a "pattern poem."

Fraser, G. S. "Skelton and the Dignity of Poetry." *Adelphi* 13 (1936):154–63. Offers a brief and hostile critique of Hawes's style.

Gordon, Ian A. "A Skelton Query." *Times Literary Supplement*, 15 November 1934, p. 795. Suggests the identification of Skelton's "Gorbellyd Godfrey" with Hawes.

Greenlaw, E., et al., eds. *The Works of Edmund Spenser*. Baltimore: The Johns Hopkins Press, 1932. Contains (1:414–18) an extended discussion of Spenser's possible debt to Hawes.

Hanson, Niels Bugge. *That Pleasant Place*. Copenhagen: Akademisk Forlag, 1973. Discusses Hawes's descriptions of gardens in the *Pastime of Pleasure*.

Hodnett, Edward. *English Woodcuts, 1480–1535.* London: Oxford University Press, 1935. This includes a discussion of the woodcuts in the *Pastime of Pleasure* and *Example of Virtue.*

Howells, Wilbur Samuel. *Logic and Rhetoric in England, 1500–1700.* Princeton, N.J.: Princeton University Press, 1956. Includes an extended examination of Hawes's discussion of rhetoric in the *Pastime of Pleasure.*

Humphreys, G. S. "Stephen Hawes." M.A. thesis, University of London, 1928. The best account of Hawes's life.

King, John N. "Allegorical Patterns in Stephen Hawes' *Pastime of Pleasure.*" *Studies in the Literary Imagination* 11 (1978):57–67. An analysis of the poem in terms of the "Herculean choice" confronting the protagonist, in particular as it affects the ending.

Knowlton, E. C. "Nature in Middle English." *Journal of English and Germanic Philology* 20 (1921):186–207. A discussion of the treatment of Nature in the *Example of Virtue* and *Pastime of Pleasure.*

Lancashire, Ian, ed. *Two Tudor Interludes: The Interludes of Youth and Hickscorner.* Manchester: At the University Press, 1980. Discusses the influence of Hawes's *Example of Virtue* on the interlude *Youth.*

Lemmi, C. W. "The Influence of Boccaccio on Hawes' *Pastime of Pleasure.*" *Review of English Studies* 5 (1929):195–98. Suggests Boccaccio's *De Genealogia Deorum* as a source for part of the *Pastime.*

Leonard, Frances McNeely. *Laughter in the Courts of Love.* Norman, Okla.: Pilgrim Books, 1981. Contains a general discussion of the *Pastime of Pleasure.*

Lewis, C[live] S[taples]. *The Allegory of Love.* London: Oxford University Press, 1936. An exploration of the treatment of allegory in the *Example of Virtue* and the *Pastime of Pleasure.*

————. *English Literature in the Sixteenth Century Excluding Drama.* London: Oxford University Press, 1954. Contains a brief but incisive overall evaluation of Hawes.

Means, Michael H. *The Consolatio Genre in Medieval English Literature.* Gainesville: University of Florida Press, 1972. Attempts very unconvincingly to argue that the *Pastime of Pleasure* is a contribution to the *consolatio* genre.

Morgan, Alice. "The Conuercyon of Swerers: Another Edition." *Library,* 5th series, no. 24 (1969):44–50. Notes the existence of a revised edition (ca. 1510) of de Worde's 1509 printing.

Murison, W. "Stephen Hawes." In *The Cambridge History of English Literature.* Cambridge: At the University Press, 1917. A discussion of all of Hawes's works, except the *Comfort of Lovers,* placing particular stress on his relationship to Spenser and his meter.

Parker, P. "Stephen Hawes." *Times Literary Supplement,* 21 June 1928, p. 468. An interpretation of lines 134–40 of the *Comfort of Lovers.*

Pearsall, Derek A. "The English Chaucerians." In *Chaucer and Chaucerians.* Edited by D. S. Brewer. London: Thomas Nelson, 1966. Includes a discussion of the *Pastime of Pleasure.*

————. *Old English and Middle English Poetry.* London: Routledge & Kegan Paul, 1977. A brief and unsympathetic discussion of Hawes's work, paying particular attention to his metrical ineptitude.

Pyle, Fitzroy. "The Barbarous Meter of Alexander Barclay." *Modern Language Review* 32 (1937:353–73. This includes a defense of Hawes's meter, arguing that it is less irregular than many of his contemporaries.

Rude, D. W. "Two Additional Allusions to Chaucer in the Works of Stephen Hawes." *American Notes & Queries* 16 (1978):82–83. Notes and discusses Hawes's references to Chaucer in the *Example of Virtue* and *Comfort of Lovers.*

Saintsbury, George. *A History of English Prosody.* 3 vols. 2d ed. London, 1908; reprint ed., New York: Russell and Russell, 1961. The first volume includes several discussions of Hawes's meter.

Schroeder, Horst. "Gerard Leigh, Stephen Hawes and the Nine Worthies." *Notes & Queries* 222 (1977):46–48. An examination of Leigh's use of the *Pastime of Pleasure* in his *Accedens of Armory.*

————. *Der Topos der Nine Worthies in Literatur und bildender Kunst.* Gottingen: Vandhoek under Ruprecht, 1971. Contains a discussion (134–38) of Hawes's presentation of the Nine Worthies in the *Pastime of Pleasure.*

Sellers, H. "Two Poems by Hawes and an Early Medical Tract." *British Museum Quarterly* 13 (1939):7–8. Announces the acquisition by the British Museum of the unique copies of the 1509 *Pastime of Pleasure* and the 1515 *Comfort of Lovers.*

Spargo, John Webster. *Virgil the Necromancer.* Cambridge, Mass.: Harvard University Press, 1934. Includes a discussion of the coarse tale of Vergil in the Godfrey Gobelive episode of the *Pastime of Pleasure.*

Warton, Thomas. *History of English Poetry.* London, 1778. This contains (in volume 2) the first extended critical discussion of Hawes's work, centering on the *Pastime of Pleasure.*

Wells, W. "Stephen Hawes and the *Court of Sapience.*" *Review of English Studies* 6 (1930):284–94. An attempt to demonstrate the influence of the *Court of Sapience* on the *Example of Virtue* and *Pastime of Pleasure.*

Wood, Anthony A. *Athenae Oxonienses.* 1691–92. 3d ed. London, 1813–20. Contains a biography of Hawes and account of the canon which includes some information not in Bale.

Woolf, Rosemary. *The English Religious Lyric in the Middle Ages.* Oxford: Clarendon Press, 1968. Includes an excellent analysis of the *Conversion of Swearers* and the tradition from which it derives.

Zander, Friedrich. *Stephen Hawes Passetyme of Pleasure verglichen mit Edmund Spensers Faerie Queene.* Rostock: Carl Hintstorff Buchdruckerei, 1905. An attempt to identify parallels between Hawes's poem and Spenser's.

Index

Aenius Sylvius, 6
Ambrose, St., 68
André, Bernard, 5
Arber, Edward, 99
Aristotle, 43
Assembly of Ladies, The, 60
Auden, W. H., 101
Augustine, St., 68

Bale, John, Bishop, 1, 2, 94
Barclay, Alexander, 6, 7, 20, 27
Bartholomaeus Anglicus, 61
Beaufort, Margaret, 6, 8, 19, 60, 63, 70
Bede, 68
Berdan, J. M., 101
Boccaccio, Giovanni, 10
Brereton, Joseph, 95, 97
Broke, Arthur, 92
Brooke, Stopford, 99
Browning, Elizabeth Barrett, 98, 102
Butler, John, 90

Campbell, Thomas, 98
Caxton, William, 12, 20
Chaucer, Geoffrey, 10, 11, 27, 89, 96, 98, 100, 105, 107
Colet, John, 9
Collins, John Churton, 100–101
Copland, Robert, 89

Cornish, William, 5
Court of Sapience, The, 28, 61

Deguileville, Guillaume de, 29–30
Dibdin, Thomas Frognall, 97
Dudley, Edmund, 56, 75

Edmund, St., 68
Edward, St., 68
Elizabeth of York, Queen of England, 4, 74, 80
Ellis, George, 97–98
Empson, Sir Richard, 56, 75
English, John, 5
Erasmus, Desiderius, 9

Feylde, Thomas, 2, 20, 89, 91
Fisher, Bishop John, 6

Gower, John, 10, 11, 27, 105, 107
Gray, Thomas, 95
Gregory, St., 68
Grocyn, William, 9

Haugh, John, 1
Hawes, Stephen: *Assembly of Ladies, The,* and, 60; Bartholomaeus Anglicus and, 61; Beaufort, Margaret, and, 6–7, 19, 63; Chaucer, Geoffrey, and, 10–11, 27; *See also*

Chaucer, Geoffrey; *Court of Sapience, The,* and, 28, 61; early life and education, 1–2, 34; Gower, John, and, 10–11, 27; *See also* Gower, John; Henry VII, and, 2, 3–8, 19, 54–56, 63, 65, 69, 70, 74–76, 105; Henry VII, and, 19, 63, 73; humanism, and, 8–10; influence, 88–94; language, 13–15, 57; Lydgate, John, and, 11–20, 27; *See also* Lydgate, John; metre, 56–57, 99–100, 102–103; posthumous reputation, 88–102; Privy Chamber, and, 3–4, 54–55, 69; Skelton, John, and, 5–8, 82, 107; *See also* Skelton, John; Worde, Wynkyn de, 20–25; *See also* Worde, Wynkyn de

WORKS:
Alphabet of Birds, 1, 2
Comfort of Lovers, 2, 3, 15, 18, 77–87, 90–91, 95, 96, 97, 101, 103, 104, 105–106, 108
Concerning the Marriage of the Prince, 1, 2
Conversion of Swearers, 17, 18, 19, 20, 23–24, 69–73, 89, 90, 99, 102, 103
Example of Virtue, 3, 4, 7, 14, 20, 22–23, 57, 59–69, 82, 91, 94, 95, 97, 103, 104, 106
Joyful Meditation, A, 18–19, 55, 56, 73–77, 99, 104
Pastime of Pleasure, The, 2, 3, 12, 14, 16, 17, 18, 20, 21–22, 24–25, 26–58, 70, 82, 89, 90, 91, 92–94, 95, 96, 97, 98, 99–100, 102, 103, 104, 106, 108

Henry V, King of England, 19, 74
Henry VII, King of England, 2, 3–10, 19, 38, 54–56, 60, 63, 65, 66, 69
Henry VIII, King of England, 8, 19, 55, 60, 63, 73, 76, 77
Herbert, George, 71
Hilton, Walter, 6
Hoccleve, Thomas, 95
Hodgson, Henry, 96–97
Holinshed, Rafael, 94

Interlude of Youth, The, 91

Jerome, St., 68

Kempis, Thomas à, 6
Knowlton, E. C., 28
Kynge Richarde, 6

Laing, David, 99
Langland, William, 98
Leigh, Gerard, 92–94
Lewis, Clive Staples, 33, 51, 94, 101–102, 103
Linacre, Thomas, 9
Lydgate, John, 2, 10, 11–20, 25, 27, 28, 30, 74, 77, 89, 95, 96, 97, 98, 99, 100, 103, 104, 105, 107

Malory, Thomas, 28
Mason, George, 95
Mead, W. E., 101, 103
Medwall, Henry, 6
Mirrour of golde for the sinful soul, The, 6
Mirror of the World, The, 28
More, St. Thomas, 6, 9, 76
Morley, Henry, 99, 102
Morton, John, Archbishop, 6

Moses, 68
Murison, W., 101

Nevill, William, 20, 91
Nine Worthies, The, 48, 49–50, 65, 104

Pearsall, Derek, 57
Pepwell, Henry, 91
Percy, Thomas, Bishop, 96
Peter, St., 68
Petrarch, Francis, 10, 49
Pilgrimage of Life, The, 29, 60, 68
Pindar, 10
Pyle, Fitzroy, 102

Quadrivium, 10, 34

Recuyell of the Histories of Troy, 28
Richard III, King of England, 4
Robinson, Ian, 101–102
Roman de la Rose, 101

Saintsbury, George, 99–100, 102
Scott, Sir Walter, 98
Seven Deadly Sins, The, 29, 31, 48, 49, 104
Seven Liberal Arts, The, 29, 33–41, 103, 104
Simnel, Lambert, 4, 65

Skelton, John, 5–6, 7–8, 9, 20, 24, 82, 96, 107
Southey, Robert, 98
Spenser, Edmund, 94, 106
Surrey, Henry Howard, Earl of, 24, 99, 107
Sydoyne and Ponthus, 28

Tottel, Richard, 90, 99
Toye, Robert, 90
Trevisa, John, 61
Trivium, 10, 34
Tudor, Mary, 81

Vergil, 43–44, 107
Vergil, Polydore, 56

Warbeck, Perkin, 4, 65
Warton, Thomas, 95–96, 97
Watson, Henry, 6
Wayland, John, 90
Wells, W., 28
Wilford, Rafe, 65
Wood, Anthony à, 12, 95
Woolf, Rosemary, 70
Worde, Wynkyn de, 6, 12, 20–25, 59, 61, 70, 88–90, 91, 101, 106
Wright, Thomas, 98–99, 101
Wyatt, Sir Thomas, 24, 99, 107

DATE DUE